When not travelling  circuit, **Damon Hill** li   and three children.

Jon Nicholson is well known for his photographic chronicles of prominent sporting personalities. His previous projects include Damon Hill's *Grand Prix Year; A Year in the Life of Linford Christie; Pole Position,* for the Williams Formula One team; and more recently a record of the England rugby team's first year in professional rugby union. Jon has also covered some of the world's most demanding sporting events, such as the Olympics, the Camel Trophy and the Paris–Dakar rally, as well as doing promotional work for companies such as Timberland and Wrangler. Married with two daughters, he lives in Haslemere, Surrey.

DAMON HILL
MY CHAMPIONSHIP YEAR

Photographs by

Jon Nicholson

WARNER BOOKS

A *Warner* Book

First published in Great Britain in 1996
by Little, Brown and Company
This edition published in 1997 by Warner Books

Text copyright © 1996 by Damon Hill
Photographs copyright © 1996 by Jon Nicholson

The moral right of the author has been asserted.

A CIP catalogue record for this book
is available from the British Library.

ISBN: 0 7515 1914 6

Typeset in Bembo by M Rules
Printed and bound in Great Britain
by Clays Ltd, St Ives plc

Warner Books
A Division of
Little, Brown and Company (UK)
Brettenham House
Lancaster Place
London WC2E 7EN

◩ CONTENTS

▦ ACKNOWLEDGEMENTS

There is no question in my mind that without the help of the following people I would not have been able to write this book about winning the world championship (if I've left anyone out, they'll have to wait for the next one): my loving wife Georgie; my beautiful children Oliver, Joshua and Tabatha; my fiercely loyal mother Bette, and sisters Samantha and Brigitte; all my friends (they know who they are); Michael and Helen Breen, for having twins just at the crucial moment; Jamie McCallum, for nearly having twins; everyone on the Hill team, the Williams team, the Rothmans team, the Renault Sport team, the Cellnet team and the Little, Brown book team; and lastly, of course, Tim Collings for wielding the tape-recorder and Jon Nicholson for his dedication to his art.

Damon Hill, November 1996

Jon Nicholson would like to thank Metro Photographic and Olympus cameras.

MY CHAMPIONSHIP YEAR

🏁 INTRODUCTION

There is no doubt that 1994 left its mark on my life. Not only did I drive through one of the most tumultuous years in the history of Formula One, experiencing at close quarters the deaths of Ayrton Senna and Roland Ratzenberger, but I also completed the year as runner-up, by the narrowest of margins, in the scrap for the world championship. It was dramatic right to the end, with the title going to Michael Schumacher after our famous coming-together in Adelaide, the final race.

That incident, of course, was the main item in the closing chapter of my last book, and the reason why I am beginning this one, principally about the 1996 season, with a reference to it. It was, unquestionably, a season of far-reaching effects; effects which stretched deep into 1995 and beyond. Quite suddenly, after Adelaide, I was much better known all over the world. At home, despite the fact that I had not won the championship, I was treated like a hero. I won the BBC Sports Personality of the Year Award, and this, along with the impact of everything else, raised my profile so much that a lot of things in my life were changed forever.

Over the winter of 1994–95, as I tried to adjust to these changes, I was heavily engaged in promotional work for the book I did in 1994 and also for Rothmans. Predictably, I found that a lot of people were very interested in the Adelaide incident; in fact, it was the main topic of conversation everywhere I went.

The Rothmans trip began immediately after Christmas and took me on a tour of Moscow, the Middle East and the Far East, lasting about two weeks. Apart from keeping me away from home, it also made me realise just how big a following Formula One has around the world. In Russia, for example, there are 100 million television viewers for each Grand Prix, and in China as many

> **Both in Russia and China there are 100 million television viewers for each Grand Prix. It is mind-boggling, when you think about it.**

again. It is mind-boggling, when you think about it.

I was certainly treated well, and given the full state-visitor treatment each time, with bodyguards and police escorts. It was the same everywhere I went, and I particularly remember arriving at Moscow airport to be taken to a room filled by fifty or so journalists. I was plunged straight into personal interviews, then taken to the city centre with a police escort, including what looked like KGB guards, and, later, a guided tour of the Kremlin and Red Square. I enjoyed it of course, but part of what was happening that winter was something new for me – a realisation that I had to get used to a new scale of recognition and a change in my relationship with the media, the public and the rest of the world.

Until then, I had been trying to get noticed. I wanted to become established as a Formula One driver with world championship potential. Quite suddenly the boot was on the other foot. I no longer needed to do anything to attract attention. Instead, somehow, I had to find a way of controlling that attention, instead of allowing it to grow and control me.

When I was in China I remember thinking, as I stood for photographs during a tour of the Forbidden City and the Great Wall, that I felt awkward and that what I was doing was trivial. But I remember also thinking that when

100 million people are interested in seeing how you're going to cope with that situation, you really do have to try and put on a good show.

The tour took me to Athens and Dubai, where I went out on the off-shore powerboats, courtesy of Rothmans; out on horseback, racing against the Russian snowmobile champion and, whenever possible, through the fitness regimes of Josef Leberer, who was always trying to get me to work in the gym. All the time I was away, I was thinking about the season ahead and how much I wanted to capitalise on the momentum I felt I had built up by the end of 1994.

Naturally I was glad to get home after the Rothmans tour. It had taken up a valuable period of time and filled up my already hectic winter schedule. In fact, that winter was so busy we didn't have time for a holiday. I seemed to get out of the car in Adelaide, after 'that' incident, and then remain active all the time until I got back in the car in March for testing. The accident in Adelaide also set the stage for 1995, because it was a controversial incident. But the underlying theme was the same as ever – it would all be about the different approaches that Michael and I took to our driving and tactics.

It seemed everyone apart from me had dwelt on the Adelaide accident and played it over and over in their minds. To me, once it was over, it was over. I was thinking more about 1995 than the past. I said to myself, 'Okay, I came close in 1994, but I think I'm on a roll and I can build on that momentum and come out stronger in 1995 – and I can do it from the word go.' So I put it all behind me. I also came out of 1994 feeling that the climax to the season was exciting, and had re-affirmed my conviction that motor racing is a worthwhile activity.

After Imola, however, I could not help but question it. What was the point? Is it frivolous? Is it right or wrong? The conclusion I came to was that, in Suzuka particularly, I had stretched myself further than ever before and had gained personal satisfaction from doing so. That assurance, in itself, gave me even more ability, untapped, and I became aware that I could use it to my advantage. In short, that race rekindled my faith in the sport, recharged my enthusiasm, and made me feel at the end of the season that I should feel completely satisfied – because I had done everything, and more, and I had not lost the championship through lack of effort. So, for myself, I had won, but it was a different kind of triumph.

But Michael was the real winner of the championship. He was the guy who scored the most points – and that was why I had nothing to do with one newspaper's idea, when I came back to London, for me being photographed with a trophy as 'the real winner of the championship'. It would have been entirely wrong. I hadn't achieved anything and I was uncomfortable, as I've said, with all the attention I was receiving. So I concentrated on 1995, when I knew Michael would be driving a new Benetton, powered, like my Williams, by a Renault engine. I felt confident too that, with all our experience, we would have the best car, that it would be competitive and reliable and Benetton would have some problems. Once the season started, I realised I could not have been more wrong. Frankly, 1995 was a year I did not enjoy.

We had David Coulthard in the team, as my team-mate, for his first full season. It was obvious he had potential and talent, but, compared to Nigel Mansell (who was expected by many to be my team-mate at one time during the winter), he was more of an unknown quantity. I was a little uncomfortable with some of his management people who, I felt, could be a little too enthusiastic in their attempts to promote David, at my expense. But otherwise we had a good relationship.

I suppose my approach to 1995 was quite simplistic. I'd come out of Adelaide the previous year with a lot of pressure on me to sell myself, sell what I was doing and promote things. I was looking for a way to cope with all that in my own style, and in the end I rejected it. After all, I am usually anti-anything. I always take the contrary position. I don't like to conform. I don't want to be told what to do. I don't want to do the expected and I have a perverse streak which, occasionally, makes me like to be difficult.

In all the pre-season hype and build-up to the 1995 season, I stuck to the one simple thing which I knew to be true – that if I worked as hard as I could to achieve one goal, then I would achieve that goal. And if I did not, then I couldn't blame myself for not trying hard enough. I thought the only thing that mattered was the result in the race and trying to do your best. For me, that was the bare essence of what it was all about. You could have as much stuff written about you as you liked, but when it came to the race it was how you performed that mattered and nothing else. That was my thinking, and I took it with me, in a very blinkered way, as my

> **Once the season started, I realised I could not have been more wrong. Frankly, 1995 was a year I did not enjoy.**

approach for 1995. Looking back, now, I realise this was naïve.

I tried to stick my head down and go in one direction, but 1995 taught me that to fight for a world title, to compete for a championship, there are many other things that you have to be able to do. These other things which seemed unimportant to me at the start of the year became more and more significant. And they had to be dealt with. However much you might not want to do it, you still have to because so many perceptions about Formula One are controlled by these outside factors rather than by performances and results. It is a sad fact, one that I did not want to acknowledge, but it is true. The thing that matters is how fast you go, but the reality, for most people, is simply what they are told – and that means my job consists of off-track things as much as on-track work.

We, the drivers, are involved in a branch of the entertainment business, not just a sport. Adelaide 1994, and the way in which 1995 finished, for me, proved this. But I went into the 1995 season in Brazil with my head down, blinkered, gambling that my results would protect me from all the other things. Regrettably, they did not.

There's no doubt it was a very tough year. This is not the place to go through it on a race-by-race basis, but I have to say that we did not have the reliability or competitiveness we needed, on a consistent basis, to do the job. The first three races of 1995 resulted in a suspension bracket breaking in Brazil, while I was leading, and then wins in Argentina and at Imola. I led the world championship for the first time and felt just great when we flew down to Barcelona for the Spanish Grand Prix. But instead of it being the start of something good, it was the start of an extended period of troubles. They went on in Monaco, Canada and France, so by the time of the British Grand Prix at Silverstone, it was a pretty tense situation for us all – and my wife Georgie was due to give birth to our third child that very weekend.

There had been a lot of advance hype, but it was nothing compared to what happened during, and then after, the race. Mostly it went pretty well, except that Michael and I were on different strategies and, after all our pit-stops, I did not actually see him. We were racing against the clock, him with one stop, me on a two-stop strategy. I was on fresh tyres, he was on old tyres and I tried to pass. We came through Bridge corner, he moved over to the right to take the left-hander, and I thought that if I stuck my car down the middle, in the gap, he would have to give way. I miscalculated. I misjudged what he was prepared to do. He is not the sort of driver who will try to avoid an accident rather than have one, and in the last few fractions of a second, this became crystal clear to me as he kept on closing the door and we collided. He knew I was there. I flatly refuse to believe he could deny knowing I was there, because I had been right behind him for the previous lap and a half. I got out of the car and kicked myself for being drawn into it, for allowing my heart to rule my head.

I was very upset, but it only got worse with the criticism in the newspapers the following day. It was a turkey shoot, and a new experience for me because the last time I had crashed with Michael I had come home and been hailed a hero. This time, I felt I was suddenly the most reviled man in England. It was a very uncomfortable feeling; I wasn't prepared for it and it took my breath away. I had to step back from it all and work out what had happened. So I went home, the baby was born and, naturally, the world returned to normal. But the season was only half-way through then, and there were plenty more unwanted experiences to come – in Germany, where another mechanical failure let me down on the first corner of the second lap; in Belgium, where Michael won from sixteenth on the grid after what I thought was an unacceptable degree of wheel-banging; in Monza, where we collided again … and so on.

The second half of the season, leading up to the Japanese Grand Prix at Suzuka, was as punishing as anything I have ever endured. The races at the Nürburgring, Aida and Suzuka all went to Michael and left me facing another barrage of criticism from the sports-writers. At one point, in Japan, I began to wonder if I was losing my marbles. My whole season, which had started so positively, had taken such a massive down-turn that I felt like packing it all in and going home.

Fortunately there were two weeks before Australia, and I spent one of them in Bali with Georgie. It was a chance to relax, to play some tennis with Mika Hakkinen, who was in the same hotel, and to determine that I would continue and that I would enjoy it. Unfortunately Mika was later to suffer severe injuries in a serious accident at Adelaide, which was another big shock, especially as we had spent time together. After Bali, I went down to Perth and spent a few days on a beach being pulverised by huge waves, and then flew to Adelaide where I turned up with more of a positive attitude. I felt a bit more immune to everything and, it seemed, the gods took pity on me too, because everyone fell off in the race and I spent seventy laps going round on my own. It was a bizarre end to a tough season; a year which taught me a lot.

I had set my expectations very high, but it had gone sour for me, very sour – and then Adelaide had saved me. I felt I could qualify on pole, enjoy myself, and soak up what was a really terrific atmosphere, and I think it helped me. It rescued me. It perked me up. I know you're only as good as your last race, your last result, so I made a big attempt to enjoy it and gave my best. I felt I had learned a lot from my mistakes, too, and I suppose it was there, in the aftermath of seeing Michael win the 1995 title, while I was being pilloried in the press, while I was recovering in Bali, that I began planning my attack for 1996.

What I had learned was that I was very fortunate to be doing a job that I enjoy, but that I had *stopped* enjoying it. The key was to learn how to enjoy it again, how to brighten it up. I am, by nature, an intense person, and I can become very obsessed with something and focus on it to the extent that I won't allow anyone or anything to intrude on that obsession. But I had learned in 1995 that this intensity only added to the pressure: it didn't do

> **I got out of the car and kicked myself ... for allowing my heart to rule my head.**

me any good to be like that or to become upset. It only made my life more difficult and so, for 1996, I decided to be more relaxed, happier and lighter. I came into racing for pleasure and I was determined to enjoy it again.

1 🏁 PRE-SEASON

After Adelaide, I was glad to get home and see the family again. I needed it. It had been a tough year and I needed to recover, to regroup, to get back to some sensible perspective on everything that had happened to me in the previous couple of months. I had taken a mauling, but my win in Australia in the final race of the 1995 season had, at the very least, left me with a good taste in my mouth for the winter.

I decided to take some time off and, looking back, it was an invaluable break. To have time at home with Georgie and the children was exactly what I needed, and I soon began to feel more like my normal self. I also began to think clearly again and to make decisions about how to tackle the new season. I felt I had to focus everything on this year, in a way that was going to be quite different from the past.

Winning in Australia had gone some way towards lifting my spirits after such a tough year. There is no doubt it was a crucial race to have won. Even then, at the end of 1995, everyone was saying how confident they felt about 1996. People started saying that 1996 was going to be a very good opportunity for me to win the championship. Ending the season with a win obviously boosted the Williams team too – it gave them something to celebrate and, like me, some laurels to rest on through the winter.

After all that, getting home was like a breath of fresh air. We'd been away for a month, for the last three races, and it was a strain going through the process of losing the championship. I'd also been away from the children throughout what was a difficult time, emotionally, and this added to the relief I felt when I finally got home to the family. It was an important period, particularly as there were a lot of other things happening in our family life just then.

About a week after I got back, for example, we moved house, finally, to the place that we'd been planning to move into all season. Unfortunately, the work had taken a lot longer than we'd expected. I'm sure it's a familiar story to anyone who has bought an older property, but quite obviously it had been an unsettling factor in the background for us all for some time. We had bought a

Victorian house in Ireland, overlooking Killiney Bay on the coast south of Dublin. It needed a lot doing to it, but we finally completed the work just before Christmas and moved in.

It is a beautiful place and, once we'd settled in, it soon made both Georgie and me feel we were in a position to go forward and make it our own – a welcome sensation after having lived in rented accommodation through virtually all of the 1995 season. We'd moved out of our previous house at the beginning of March and, in all, we'd moved home three times in eighteen months. But this was different – this was permanent. So, even before Christmas, there was a sense of optimism at home, a feeling that things were going in the right direction. It was a satisfying moment. I knew what it meant to Georgie and to the children, but I also knew too that it would help me, my fitness programme and my driving. This was

> **Sometimes you eat some food from which you have no ill effects, but which causes a reaction in your system that can have a harmful effect on your performance.**

because one of the developments we had decided upon for the new house was to have a gym installed, to allow me to do more training and to stay at home and therefore save time. This was a crucial decision because, throughout the winter, I was able to train at home and prepare myself really well for the new season. After Adelaide, we did only two tests, and before Christmas I had the long break I wanted, which thoroughly refreshed me. It gave me a proper rest and rekindled my enthusiasm. But, crucially, it made want to get back into a racing car.

It didn't take me long before I began to feel the urge to get back in the cockpit again and to do it right in 1996. But Christmas at home, in our new house, came first, and it was a very good family experience and a great success. We had all our relatives to stay: my sisters and their husbands; my mother; Georgie's mother; everyone. It was hard work, of course, being the host, but it actually went well. I was amazed. Then, soon afterwards, I took my son Joshua off skiing, which I managed to fit into a trip which I knew I had to make for a fitness assessment. This was to examine my physical and medical condition completely, and it was part of a programme instigated by Erwin Göllner, the team's, and my, new physio-trainer.

Erwin had been taken on by Frank Williams, the team owner, after some persuasion from our technical director

Patrick Head, to take the responsibility for keeping the drivers in tip-top shape. We had lost Josef Leberer, who had been Ayrton Senna's guy from the year before, and it was necessary to get an experienced trainer on board. Erwin was just the man. So off I went to Austria, where I spent a day in a clinic having needles stuck in my ear to measure my lactic acid level, and running on a treadmill to the point of complete exhaustion. Then they took readings from it to assess my aerobic fitness level.

In addition to that, they did sprint testing and reaction testing, which meant I had to respond to a computer image by moving my hands. This was to show how fast my mind reacted to visual stimuli, and how fast I responded. On that test I came top out of 25,000 sports people they had tested, including tennis players, skiers and all sorts of others. That was also very encouraging.

It was just part of the preparation for the fitness programme I was planning, to try and improve everything I possibly could. I wanted to give myself the very best chance of coming out at the start of the season in perfect shape and of improving on that during the year. This data was important. It was something to refer back to during the season. Another part of the test was to analyse my blood to reveal if I had any allergies, which were not previously apparent, and to make sure, as a result, that I ate the right food on race day, my performance day.

Sometimes you eat some food from which you have no ill effects, but which causes a reaction in your system that can have a harmful effect on your performance. Only by a small percentage, perhaps, but it can be a factor – and reducing that factor means you can improve your alertness and sharpness quite significantly. All these little things were vital to me if I wanted to be at my best.

After the tests, I went off with Joshua and some friends and their sons to Karl-Heinz Zimmerman's house, in Lech, where I spent a fantastic four or five days langlaufing – cross-country skiing – and relaxing. Karl-Heinz is one of the great characters in Formula One. He runs the Rothmans motor-home at all the Grands Prix; suffice to say his hospitality is second to none. I had never been langlaufing before in my life, but that didn't bother me at all, so I rented a pair of skis and tried to remember what I could of watching this sport on television.

I got up early. In fact, on a couple of days, it was too early and they hadn't yet unlocked the place, so I had to climb out of the window. I langlaufed up and down some very scenic routes through the forests, beside the mountains, beside the river, all on my own. It was not so much a piste as a track, but it was very beautiful. I was there long before anyone else. The solitude was very good for my mind, and the exercise was very good for both my mind and my body. I used to go for an hour or so, and it was a brilliant exercise; I really enjoyed it – although, on one occasion, I did have a bit of a fright coming down a hill, when I failed to negotiate a corner, and nearly went through a fence. I remember thinking, as I tumbled down the road, 'How can I explain *this*?' Imagine if I had broken some bone. It would have been a bit akin to tripping over a step. Quite apart from that, there was no one around at that time of the morning, so if I'd broken my leg I could have lain there for hours. But the experience was truly exhilarating, and it made me understand a lot more about the fitness of the really top guys in skiing.

On top of all that, Joshua learned to ski, which was another personal delight for me. I learned to ski at the age of five on wooden skis and wearing leather boots, in the early 1960s, when it was a bit of a novelty to go skiing at all. With Joshua, I was amazed. They put him into the Austrian ski school and, at first, he didn't want to know. Why did he have to wear these horrible boots? Why did he have to clomp around trying to hold on to his skis? He was pretty cheesed off. But three days later he won a medal for going down a slalom course.

He was going up and down the button lift on his own and telling me how to do it, then he was coming down the mountain and saying: 'Look, Daddy, this is how you do it!' The speed at which children learn to ski is incredible, and I was very pleased to have been there with him. I'd taken him away for a day or so before, but I'd never been away and looked after him like that for four or five days. It was quite an experience and I got to know him much better – but still had to remind myself, 'Wow, he's only five.' He is so little. At home, I expected him to be able to do almost anything, but put into another context, I suddenly realised how young he was.

It wasn't his first experience of speed. We've had one or two things at home – pedal cars and so on – and he once came down a flight of stairs on a sledge. It was unintentional, and mercifully he was unhurt. He is quite a character. He tells me to keep both hands on the wheel when I'm driving, and stuff like that. But he's got flair, no question. We went tobogganing and he loved it. Some children, I realised, like the speed thing and have an affinity with it, and he seems to be one of them.

Over the winter, I really felt I had spent some time with my family, so I didn't feel quite as guilty about going away so much when the season came round again – I felt I was putting everything in place. The children were going to school regularly and settling in, and Georgie was happy because the home was coming together.

I was also able to train regularly and get my affairs in order, partly by taking on additional people to help me cope with the huge interest I was subject to because of the popularity of the sport. I organised myself, my office and my personal affairs better. I found time to catch my breath. Consequently, I went into the first part of pre-season testing better prepared than I had ever been before, and this gave me a lot of confidence. Also, I didn't get involved in any world tours for sponsors; I just stayed close to home and concentrated on the things that mattered to me for 1996.

One of the decisions which helped me was to take on a PR agency, to distinguish between the good and the bad when it came to personal appearances and so on. I also needed help just to cope, quite simply, with the sheer volume of requests. It was a good situation to be in, being able to pick and choose, but I wanted to make sure that I was better understood and able to get across to the world a more accurate picture of the real me. I felt I'd been misunderstood in 1995. I also wanted to be relieved of a lot of the pressure.

One example of the success of this new set-up was the opportunity to do the Pizza Hut commercial. Of course,

I was paid very nicely, thank you, but that wasn't the only reason I did it. I also wanted to show that I could enjoy a laugh at my own expense. I thought the commercial was successful and very funny, and I got a lot of good reactions to it. For those who didn't see it, the joke is basically that I finish second in a pizza-eating contest – to Murray Walker, the BBC's long-serving and famous television commentator. As he finishes off his pizza, he screams something like, 'And Hill finishes second! Again!', in typical Murray style, and I lose my rag and grab him by the lapels and then he shouts, 'And Damon Hill has lost it, he's lost control!' and so on. The humour was all at my own expense, but it showed I could take it on the chin.

Another good thing about that commercial was that it made people smile. Obviously, I take my job very seriously – I am often told that I take it too seriously, in fact; that I have a furrowed brow and an intense look on my face too often – but I know it is also important to enjoy my job. Naturally I want to do my best, but I realised

> **The humour was all at my own expense, but it showed I could take it on the chin.**

during the run-up to the start of the season that I also needed to relax and share my feelings a little more.

All in all, I felt far more relaxed and confident than I had done before, and I knew that I was achieving the sort of feeling I wanted to have on the run-in to the new season. I had done a little testing with the old car, but my main concern was to get my hands on the new one. There was nothing for me to prove in driving the old car, but when I did, at Estoril, I was quick – and that confirmed to me that my approach was right and that I had made the correct decision in giving myself some time and space away from it all after the previous season. Returning to the car and then driving with a fresh mind, it was amazing to discover how much more receptive I was to things I had not been receptive to before. I knew, on reflection, that I had been bombarded too much in the past, and I was right to have changed my approach.

Another change, during the winter, was that of my race engineer. My previous engineer had been David Brown, but he left to join McLaren, after a long association with the team. It meant an important appointment had to be made, and the team decided to promote from within by giving the job to Tim Preston. He had worked previously in the drawing office and in the factory, but he had not engineered a car before. This meant that I had to help him, and together we had to find our feet. I think it was a good thing for me; I had to take more responsibility and I wanted to make sure that the relationship worked well.

The engineer is an important, very important, guy. He is the interface between a very subjective thing – the driver – and a completely objective thing – the car and the mechanics. I realised this and I wanted to get everything right between us. It is completely futile to regard a driver as an exact piece of the equation, because every driver has his own interpretation of what, for example, understeer or oversteer actually is. Factually, it may be proven, but to what degree? How can a driver establish this and explain it? There are so many variables, all relative to the driver. Some drivers will drive with outrageous amounts of understeer which others couldn't cope with at all – so the engineer has to understand the driver and his language. As a result, there is a process, during the preliminary period, when a driver is feeling his way with a new engineer.

That's how it was with Tim, though I felt it was necessary for me, in many ways, to take more charge of the running of the car. I learned a lot more because of this, as I was able to do things differently from the way they were done before, with David Brown, when many things were seen as fixed items. For example, I was able to say, 'No, let's see this differently' – and whether it was brake temperatures or tyre pressures or whatever, it gave me some freedom and some feeling about which way to go. Working with a new engineer – while staying in very close contact with Adrian Newey, our chief designer – gave me a new perspective and another source of positive energy and interest.

In fact, the whole subject of engineers and their relationships with teams and drivers is a fascinating and ever-changing area in our sport. It used to be much simpler and easier to understand than it is today, when we have teams of designated data analysts to interpret everything we do on the track. But you still need the driver – he's the only person who can identify a squiggly line on a screen and say, 'Oh, I know that one – that's when I went over the kerb – it's not the dampers or anything.' In the end, a lot of it is subjective to the driver's wants and needs. The data can tell you things, but you need to be able to look at it and make it work for you in setting the car up better for the way you want to drive it.

It is all quite a complex operation and it needs a team approach. It can't be done by just one person; there are too many disciplines. But it is a part of the job which fascinates me, as I love tinkering and sorting things out.

There is nothing more satisfying than to tweak something and find it works ten times better than it did. You may find there's a part of the track that you couldn't drive flat-out, but after a change on the car you suddenly go flat-out straight through it. You can see the results instantly on a stopwatch (or a 'computerised timing monitor'!) and it is that which is the reward for thinking so hard and solving the problem. I really enjoy it; it helps me to understand that mysterious thing which is sometimes called a brilliant car, and sometimes called something quite different. But it is all so subjective, so elusive. The sun comes out and a brilliant car is suddenly no good … why?

Working with the engineers is part of the job; an important and satisfying part of the job – and good fun. I knew that, and that's why I worked at my relationships with everyone during the pre-season testing. Sometimes I'd go back to the hotel, after a day in the car, have a workout and something to eat, and then go back to the track because something had struck me while I was on the exercise bike. I'd stay until my eyelids started to fall and then I'd be away to bed and up again the next day and straight back to the car. I've always worked hard, and I enjoy thrashing through problems to get to the bottom of them. That is how I went about things in testing.

It was all part of my refreshed approach to the season. I knew another senior engineer was due to join the team too – James Robinson, who used to work with Ayrton Senna at McLaren – and I was keen to see us all working together in a successful and efficient manner. Part of my winter agenda had been to talk to Frank Williams and Patrick Head about how I felt these things could be improved, from my own point of view, and they listened very carefully. I wanted to galvanise a new approach, to try and get away from the manner in which the team had always gone about their racing. We needed some new direction, and I was pleased at the way in which my thoughts were received. It gave me another reason to be optimistic.

As a result of all this, we were working on our preparations more intensively, I think. We practised our pit-stops a lot in the winter. Carl Gaden, our chief mechanic, took more and more responsibility for the working of the pit-stops, and we worked on them together. We discussed the issue in real detail, and I came away from all this feeling we were heading into the new season as the slickest operating team in Formula One. Testing had given us a chance to examine that feeling, and the results were pretty good. We all felt that we knew what we wanted and where we were going.

In pre-season testing at Estoril there was great enthusiasm and determination. I worked very hard, particularly with Tim, but also with Adrian, as we all wanted to assess the new car as comprehensively and as quickly as possible. On one day I did 101 laps of Estoril – which is something of an achievement and pretty tough for both car and driver – but I got out at the end of the day and didn't feel the slightest bit worn out. And the car ran reliably. Once again, I felt all the ingredients for success were there.

But I was not, of course, the only man in the Williams garage looking to enjoy a successful year in the drivers' championship. Jacques Villeneuve had made it plain from his arrival that he was not in Formula One for the ride, but wanted to win races and titles. We didn't know each other well at the start, but the pre-season promotional work gave us an ideal opportunity to spend time together in a more sociable situation than usual. Apart from the many photographs which had to be taken of the car and the drivers and the team, we were both involved in a special pre-season television event organised by Rothmans. This meant a complete day of testing was put aside so that, it seemed, thousands of journalists from all around the world could ask the same questions over and over again.

The whole thing lasted from nine in the morning to

five in the evening, and we sat in a garage and talked, via a satellite link-up, with these reporters who were sitting in their own countries. We began in New Zealand and worked west – and it seemed a long way to go in a single day like that! It did, however, give me a chance to chat with Jacques quite a bit. He was asked questions about what he thought of me and I was asked what I thought of him and, put on the spot like that, we had to come up with something reasonably honest. It gave us a good chance to develop an understanding.

I soon realised that Jacques was a very easy-going guy who liked a laugh and a joke. He was also very honest, and pretty direct, too. One of the first things I liked about him was that he would come to ask me what my car was doing wrong, because if his was doing the same we could both go to Patrick or Adrian and prove we had a real problem. Quite often, in some teams, you just don't get the honesty which enables you to make that kind of progress. My respect for Jacques grew a lot over the testing period, because he is not a novice in any way at all, and that was apparent. He had come to Formula One from IndyCars in the United States, where he had won everything, and he had a very good handle on being in the limelight and also on setting up a car and racing it. I took a close look at him and gauged from what he did in testing how I thought he would perform in the season. From that alone, I realised he would be a very strong competitor. All the hype may have been about how I would be the favourite for the championship – and obviously I was happy to go into the season thinking I was the one to beat – but it would have been wrong for me to come out saying I was going to win everything. I knew, from 1995, just how tough it could be.

My main line with the media pre-season was to stress the level and the depth of the competition around. It was difficult for me to impress that on many people, because it was easy for them to think that if I had come second last time, and had the best car now, then it was logical that I would win the title. But my experience told me that life is just not like that, so I felt I was treading water through testing, just waiting and seeing how things were panning out. I wanted to keep things sensible and remind people of the reality.

I knew I had a team-mate who was very hungry for success. I knew Benetton had two extremely competent drivers with the same engines as us. I knew Ferrari would be the wild card, with the world champion Michael Schumacher, my main rival from the past two seasons, in a car of unknown potential but sure to be in the equation. It would be a threat, sooner or later, and so too would

McLaren. In testing, they looked very good. Mika Hakkinen came straight back after recovering from his accident and was quick immediately. The Jordans went very well in testing too, so I was prepared to face a big challenge. I concentrated on keeping fit, staying out of trouble, and just weighing things up as the season's opening race in Melbourne got nearer and nearer. This time I wanted to be ready for anything.

> **" ... it was easy to think that if I had come second last time, and had the best car now, then it was logical that I would win the title. But my experience told me that life is just not like that ... "**

2 🏁 AUSTRALIA

I packed up early at the final test. The car had to be flown home, stripped down and prepared – and after ten days of non-stop work at Estoril, I was ready to go too. It was another long spell away from home, and, as always, I was glad to get back even if I knew it was only to be for a few days. Three, to be precise. Then I was away again to Paris to make a promotional appearance for Elf, followed by two more days at home and the long flight to Australia. It was an exciting time, and I was greatly looking forward to the new season, but I also knew we were approaching the really hard graft again – the intensive periods of activity, the long spells away from home and the special difficulties that go with that, the testing to follow, the constant travel, the PR work. All of it. Yet, overall, I was very optimistic about the car and about the season ahead.

Actually I love the travel; don't let me give the wrong impression. Each time I walk into an aeroplane I think, 'Great – I'm going somewhere!' and I really do get a tremendous buzz out of it. But often I also feel, to quote Bill Bryson, that I'm 'neither here nor there', and that can be a bit disorientating, particularly on a first-of-the-season trip as long as the one to Australia.

I knew we had accomplished a lot in testing. I knew about the car. I felt we had prepared properly, worked out the team's operations and paid proper attention to all the other aspects of the job, like dealing with the media. The more you drive, the more you learn about your own strengths and weaknesses and what makes a car go well. I felt more complete: better adapted to the job in every respect and confident that I could do things my own way. In my mind, I felt ready, and I was able to reflect with some satisfaction on my preparations as I made the long journey to Melbourne.

Looking back, I realised my life had turned into a kind of tornado. One minute, it seemed, I was living in relative peace in Wandsworth; the next, I was fighting to win the world championship and attracting a lot of attention. If it had all happened to me when I was younger, I might have taken to it more quickly, but because it happened relatively late in my life, even though it was something I had been aiming for, it was more difficult to understand. I found it difficult to get out of the habit of thinking, 'Oh, I'll just pop out and do some shopping' or 'I'll wait here for a moment, to see if my friend turns up'. That was just not possible anymore.

If I stand anywhere now, for any length of time, a crowd gathers. It's a very strange business, but it's something I've had to learn to come to terms with in the last few years. Now, I think I have finally come to grips with the concept of Damon Hill – Racing Driver.

I was approaching my fourth season with the Williams team. I had grown up with them, in Formula One terms. I felt more a part of the team and I knew things were shaping up right: they knew me, I knew them, and we appreciated each other's respective strengths and weaknesses. There was no bull between us. We'd all had several downers together, some pretty heavy moments, as well as some good ones. And, from the top of the business down, everyone felt we should get back to enjoying what we

> **The more you drive, the more you learn about your own strengths and weaknesses and what makes a car go well.**

were doing. That, after all, is partly why we were all there: we all liked motor racing, and we knew it wasn't worth doing if it was going to be agony all the way.

We'd had several sit-downs together, real heart-to-heart discussions, over the winter, and I'd been to see Frank Williams, feeling it was important to sort some things out. I was there on factory visits and we chatted about how things could have gone better. We tried to clear up where we both stood, and Frank was very understanding and positive. Sometimes, he'll just phone me up to see how Georgie and the children are. He has got to know me better and better. We knew each other well from the last three years and he has always been, at crucial times, the guy to have a quiet word and tell me what he thinks. I value that a great deal.

At the end of the day, he is the boss. He's seen a lot of races and drivers and doesn't give much away, but you know that when he does say something, it is the product of vast experience gleaned from racing through all these years. Having said that, he would confess readily that he knows nothing about how to make a car go quicker, the mechanics of it. That's not his job — that's why he has Patrick and Adrian there. But he does know about racing drivers.

That is why Jacques came into the team. He brought

something fresh with him. I would never want to be negative about David Coulthard, in any way, because we were getting on much better towards the end of 1995 than we had done before, and I think I had a much better understanding of him, but Jacques' outlook was very positive and healthy. He was quite happy to get on with the job and work together. His attitude was simply that whoever drove better in the race deserved the better result.

Jacques sees it as a competition, a sport, which is to be won and lost fairly, and he enjoys what he does. He has a very 'up' personality, and that was welcome. David was pretty upbeat too, but through no fault of his own he joined the team at a difficult time, whereas Jacques joined during a far less intensive period – I think my mood was lighter, too. I think the team found my intensity quite difficult at times, and often thought I was cheesed off about something, whereas, in actual fact, all my intensity came from a straightforward desire to get a good result – for them as much as for me.

So, I made a conscious effort this year not to let anyone be affected by my mood quite so much. If you are confident and relaxed, then it will rub off on them. I wanted to be positive and in a good frame of mind, and that was how I approached things when I flew to Sydney to finish my preparations for the opening race.

Over the winter, there was a lot of talk about me being a changed man, but it had really happened at the previous year's Australian Grand Prix. Frank Williams had said it then and, in a sense, it was true. When I was in Bali, before the Adelaide race, I realised I had some fantastic friends around me, people I could really rely on. In the past, I had done everything on my own and pushed people away, but I realised I could draw on them. There was no one single thing that happened. I relaxed and thought about everything and spent some time with Georgie. Without question, she is far and away the single most important adult person in my life. She is my antithesis, everything that I am not; in fact she's so different from me I often wonder how we got together! We don't like the same music; she likes to do nothing, where I like to go around and do as many things as I can; she likes relaxing, where I like to be active all the time. But we hit it off in a different way, and when I tend to go to an extreme in one direction, I spend time with her and she shows me the alternatives, the flip-side. It's like taking a pill or something, and it has a great effect on me.

She makes me spend time with the children. And, if you get two days with the children, consecutively, or even three days, things start to take on a different momentum and a different pace. She also makes sure I spend time with my friends. It is important to me to be with people I like and trust. This may sound like an obvious thing to say, but sometimes it is difficult to see things clearly and in perspective when there's so much pressure building up during a season.

One member of my 'team', for example, is Michael Breen. He is my solicitor, and has worked on every business deal and contract I have done since 1985. He was responsible for negotiating my contracts with Frank, and he also has a fantastic outlook on life. Michael is from Northern Ireland, has a great sense of balance and is just one of a group of very close friends who help me. He and Jon Nicholson, another close friend (and the photographer for this book), came to the Adelaide race last season, meeting me beforehand in Perth, after I had been in Bali. We played on surfboards and generally messed around; it was excellent, great fun. I really enjoyed it – it blew away all the cobwebs and did me a lot of good, as I think my performance in Adelaide proved.

I'd never been to Sydney before, but like everyone else I'd heard a lot about it. I knew I needed to be in Australia early, well in advance of the race, to get over the jet lag, so it was a perfect opportunity to go there. They say it takes an hour a day to recover, and I think that's probably about right. So, with eleven hours' time difference, I needed to be there eleven days before, but there just wasn't that much time so I arrived on Friday, nine days before the race and, together with some friends, spent a few days going round the city, looking at the harbour and the sights. It is a wonderful place. The sun shines, the boats look beautiful and it is a very attractive city, with a great atmosphere. It has a lot of quaint Regency-style buildings, which look as if they might have been in Brighton before being transported half-way around the world to end up in this semi-tropical paradise.

Remembering Perth from the year before, I decided it would be a good idea to get back to the surf, so I travelled north of Sydney and found some superb beaches. I'm sure it did me good to enjoy myself before Adelaide and Melbourne, and I wonder if the fact that I went surfing before winning both races isn't entirely coincidental! I felt completely invigorated and in good shape when the time came to head down to Melbourne. It was a new place, a new track, a new season and I was ready for it.

The first thing I did on arriving was to check out the new circuit to see what we'd let ourselves in for. I was pleased to see they'd done a good job, the layout was pretty forgiving in most places. There were one or two things I didn't like, but I went to see the new administrator for circuit safety, Admiral Roger Lane-Knott, who was very much on the case with all the things which needed to be done. In fact, they made quite a lot of modifications to the circuit before the race meeting started, and it all looked much safer. I am happy to say, too, that one of my suggestions was taken on board: there was one corner – the third from last, a right-hander – where I asked them to put in a lot more tyres, and they did. They had more accidents there than at any other corner. I lost count of the number of cars which went off into the wall, which would have had no tyres against it if nothing had been done.

It was good to be back in a real race atmosphere again. For all the hype and pre-season conjecture, the great thing at last was that we were now getting to the moment of truth. I think all drivers like to get to that moment, because nobody knows what's going to happen and we can only guess at what the car is really like. Testing can be misleading – only a race can tell you the truth.

There is always a buzz that goes through you when you get to the first race. At the circuit, there was a familiar atmosphere. It was almost as if we were back in Adelaide from the previous year. There was a great deal of interest in both myself and Jacques. It built up right through the week. A lot of the journalists who were fans of his father were still around, and there was a lot of affection felt for him because it was his first Formula One race – and, boy, did he get off to a good start. He just went out and served notice that he was there to win. I thought it was a clear warning to me that the guy was good, and really up for it. In some ways, though, this was a good thing, because it shifted the spotlight away from me for the time being.

If Jacques hadn't done so well, the team would have been relying solely on my efforts. His performance meant there was a little shared responsibility, and while I would never want to settle for second best to anyone, I knew too that he had given hope to the team, a belief that we had not one but two drivers in with a shout for the championship. However, that doesn't mean I was happy for him to take pole position from me when he did!

At the time, he was quite a way back on the grid and I was ahead of Michael on pole and thinking, 'Here we go, it's going to be me and Michael again this year' when wham! In the last minute, he put in a quick lap time and did a brilliant job in his first qualifying. That is when I used my special word to make me feel better: 'bollocks'. I said it to myself in my crash helmet. Then I got out and smiled and congratulated him – but, all the time, I was swallowing my pride, kicking myself and saying, 'You let that one through the net there.' But you have to give him credit. Jacques did a great job and made a great start.

I knew my car hadn't felt absolutely right, not perfect, during those first couple of days, so I made a small adjustment to it for race day. It was one of those things you do when you sit down with the engineers (in my case Adrian and Tim). You spend a lot of time at the circuit, you go through everything, and a picture emerges. I made these changes because I just did not feel I could complete a race distance easily with the car handling the way it was. The changes worked, it came in fantastically and the car was absolutely beautiful in the warm-up on Sunday, when I was quickest. I knew, if it stayed like that, that I was in very good shape.

For the Melbourne race we had a new start system. This involved five red lights going on, and then all of them going off simultaneously. When they all go off, that's when you are supposed to go; there were no green lights anymore. The reason this new system was brought in was that in a couple of races over the last few years a green light had failed to come on when it was supposed to – and nobody had known what to do. So they decided

> **You spend a lot of time at the circuit, you go through everything, and a picture emerges.**

to get rid of the greens, and simply to start when the reds go out.

At the first start I was caught out completely. We'd been given several briefings, but my mind, for some reason, hadn't taken it all in. As I sat there at the start, I was still in the old automatic 'green-light-go' mode. I sat there on the grid and they all went off – and I was still looking for a green light! Obviously, I made a dreadful start.

I slipped well back, while Jacques got off the line cleanly, and I also got myself on to the dirt going into the first corner. I nearly lost it. Both Ferraris went through and I just thought to myself, 'Okay, hang on here kid, it's not over yet … but it's going to be hard getting it back from here.' And then they stopped the race.

Martin Brundle had had a huge accident, from which he was lucky to escape unhurt, and it meant I was able to have a lucky escape too. You can never count on that sort of thing happening. I had another chance, and I made sure that this time I got it right. I slotted in behind Jacques and that's where I stayed for the whole race. I just sat behind him. I had a few goes at him, here and there, but it was obvious he was going to make it damn near impossible to get past. I decided to wait for the pit-stops.

My strategy had been to go on as long as I could,

because it was a one-stop race for us. Michael, contrary to our predictions that he would go for a one-stop race as well, had gone for a two-stop strategy. So, for the first half of the race, he was right on my tail. I was thinking he wasn't doing too badly for someone in a new car which had had so many problems, and kept an eye on my old adversary, very closely, until the first pit-stop. Then, sure enough, I knew it was just going to be between Jacques and me because of Michael's early stop.

My plan was to go a bit further than Jacques. I thought that would give me an opportunity to go past because, while I was light on fuel and he was heavier, I'd be able to go quicker for two laps and then come in and refuel ahead of him. In fact, that is what happened, except that I was held up in a gaggle of cars and didn't manage to gain as much time as I'd hoped – so although I was ahead of him, I wasn't that far ahead.

It meant it was pretty tight. We had an exciting moment, where I didn't defend the line in one of the

> **Then, sure enough, I knew it was just going to be between Jacques and me because of Michael's early stop.**

corners and ran a bit wide, and he came through and fought back and regained the lead. At that point I thought to myself, 'Well, there's a long way to go yet …' We were only half-way through the race, so I just sat back and watched him a bit more. He was really pushing, and I decided I had to get a little bit closer and put more pressure on him, and see how it went.

I had quite a few laps to do this in – about twenty at that time – and I thought he was bound to make a mistake somewhere. Then, going into the first corner, he got on to some bumps, over-braked, got on the grass and just as I was coming round, came back on to the track. If I'd kept my foot down he'd have come back on the track and hit me, so I had to lift off and then get on the gas again while he re-positioned himself on the circuit. Then he came across again, and I had to lift off again! It was a pretty hairy moment; very exciting.

Nevertheless, I did get a chance to get outside him at the next corner, and having previously defended on that inside line, on cold tyres, I thought there was a chance he might not be able to brake as late again. That would have given me the line and I would have been able to get him on the outside. I tried it, but he gave me the biggest chop you could imagine, but we did not touch. There is a big difference between chopping someone and hitting them, and I knew again it was time for me to let sense prevail, because I could see this guy was going to hang on to his lead with everything he had. He had an opportunity to win his first Grand Prix and he really wanted to do it, so I knew I was going to have to sit back and wait for an opportunity with the back-markers later in the race.

I was right to wait, but for a different reason, as it turned out. When we got the cars back, afterwards, we discovered that when Jacques had his 'moment' and went off across the grass, the floor of his car had taken a wallop and a joint on an oil pipe had been dislodged. For those final twenty laps or so, as I sat behind him, I had oil sprayed all over me. There was a lot of it – so much, in fact, that it was coming down the inside of my visor. It was so bad I couldn't wipe my visor any more and could barely see where I was going. My car was covered in it. I'd never seen anything like it before.

I could see the oil was coming from his car, so I got on the radio to Adrian Newey and told him there was something wrong with Jacques' car. He said they knew and were telling him to slow down. They actually said that before the incident they'd been asking him to back off because they felt he'd looked a bit wild in some of his manoeuvres – and they were concerned we would both get in a tangle.

That gave me even more to worry about. As the laps were reeled off less and less oil appeared, but that left three potential problems for the team: firstly, that I might go off by skidding on his oil; secondly, that his engine might fail and cause him to break down; and thirdly, that I might go off and then he might break down. Facing a possible scenario of two cars not finishing, I decided I was not going to back off. If I'd dropped back he would have had an easy time and cruised to the win. So, I had to sit on his tail, as close to him as I could, and get covered in this gunk while the team tried to communicate with Jacques over the radio. Eventually, they gave him a slow signal when his oil pressure began dropping. He had virtually none left at the finish – it was all over me and my car!

So Jacques had to fall back and that, really, was it. I won the first race of the season, became the first man to win two consecutive Grands Prix in the same country, and I led the world championship! I can honestly say I really felt I deserved to win. Everyone was disappointed for Jacques, and he was disappointed too. After the race, I said to him, 'Bloody good race, mate. Well done. I am sorry for you that your car broke down.' He took it well.

It was a very exciting finish. I felt I did the job, drove

well, had the race under control. I didn't get involved in any tangles and came home with ten points – and it was like breathing fresh air for the first time in a long time. But, of course, it was only one race – there were still fifteen more to go.

3 🏁 BRAZIL & ARGENTINA

After Australia I went to Hong Kong for a day of promotional work for Rothmans, which involved doing four or five interviews for television companies in that part of the world, like Star TV, and then posing for some pictures at a golf club. For me it meant hard work, not much enjoyment and a delay before I could return home. By the time I got on the plane I was dog-tired, but at the same time I had a feeling of great satisfaction because I was going home as the winner of the opening race of the season, which can really help take the tedium out of a fourteen-hour flight.

We didn't do any testing between then and Brazil because the only cars we had were the ones we'd raced in Australia, and they were being shipped back to the UK. So we had three weeks off – and, as usual, I got back home and immediately went down with a cold. Apparently this is quite common after a long flight and a big time-zone change. It put me out of action for a week or so, but afterwards I was able to get into some serious training with Erwin. I'd arranged for him to come over to Ireland during the middle week of the three, and I made sure we did some really intensive work because I knew that the next race, in Brazil, was going to be very physical.

The Interlagos circuit, at São Paulo, is one of the hardest tracks on the Grand Prix circuit. It is very bumpy, and left-handed – most of the time we're turning right, and because our bodies are less used to turning left we find it tough. From my experience of racing there in the past, I found it put quite a strain on my neck. Even people like Ayrton Senna, who you would never see wearing a neck brace at any other track, wore one in Brazil, with a hook from the crash helmet to his arm. If you decide to wear one, it means you can't hold your head up freely, which was a bit of a problem for me, since it always puts me off. I just can't drive with any kind of neck strap, so I had to train extra hard to deal with the problems of racing on a left-hand circuit.

Erwin came over to Ireland to set up some training specifically for this problem. He had designed and built a machine, like a cockpit simulator, with a seat from my racing car. It was very basic, bolted in a frame with a steering column and the steering wheel I use when I'm driving. It had a lever on the end, and Erwin put weights on the steering while I tried to turn it. We adjusted the weights and did different numbers of repeats. We also put a hook on the crash helmet and had a system of pulleys and weights, so I could lift weights up with my neck and turn the steering wheel at the same time. It simulated, as best we could, the action of driving. It was an important exercise for me, as I could mentally test myself – as if in a race – as well as physically improve my condition. I like to do a lot of training before a race, so I am convinced of my own capabilities and performing at 100 per cent throughout the meeting. After winning in Australia, recovering from my cold and training really well, I felt I was bang in top form before I left for Brazil.

I flew out of London on the Tuesday before the race, arriving on Wednesday. It is a long flight, but not such a big time change, and with the extra night in hand I decided it was time to have a group celebration. I took the team out to one of Brazil's fantastic *churascerias*, high-class meat restaurants, at the height of the mad-beef scare in Britain – at home, everyone was in the grip of the panic about eating meat, and here they were dishing up the finest cuts of Brazilian beef in the most delicious way! I very rarely eat red meat, especially before a race meeting, but I had to try some and it was quite superb. There were all these mechanics, who'd been put off eating beef back at home, tucking in with gusto. We had a great evening, and after that we went on to one of São Paulo's many night-clubs.

In the team there are some people who have been to Brazil a few times, and they know the best, and the worst, places to visit. They explained that there were some high-class places to go and some low-class ones, so I said we should start at the bottom and work our way up. As soon as we got to the first place, the club owner recognised me and, much as I tried to keep a low profile, I ended up signing autographs for everyone. While this was going on, there was a show on the dance-floor which definitely wouldn't be seen on British television, even after nine o'clock, and yet my engineer and some other guys from the team managed to spend the entire time talking about cars, serial numbers, Cortina Mark 7s and Capris and so on and so on. They just didn't seem to notice, or care about, anything going on around them. I was flabber-gasted that this was their overriding interest at a time like that, but if you ever needed proof that some men are interested only in machinery this was the perfect example.

It didn't take me long to feel I'd had enough of the attention I'd attracted and I soon left for the hotel. It had been a good night out, and the atmosphere in the team, having won the last race, was excellent. It all went towards improving the feel-good factor for everyone, and the following day we all got back to our work with a real vengeance. Everyone in the team has a job to do and they all do it brilliantly; they certainly did a first-class job in Brazil, in every way.

I don't think anyone can visit Brazil without being amazed. I cannot go there without thinking about the kind of pressure that Ayrton Senna must have been under, as a megastar in a country like that. He was extremely wealthy by anyone's standards, but when you're in Brazil and you see the level of the problems they face, with something like 25 million people living in São Paulo alone, one-third of the people in Rio living in *favelas*, and the general poverty everywhere, it really makes you stop and think. We take part in an event which, in every respect, could be described as frivolous or unnecessary compared to the scale of Brazil's problems. The ticket prices are astronomical, out of reach for at least 95 per cent of the population, but life goes on and the Brazilians have a fantastic desire to enjoy life to its fullest. It shed some light, for me, on how and why Ayrton was apparently so statesmanlike – he had to be. He represented hope to millions of Brazilians, and that was a hell of a responsibility.

This year, we were there again to entertain, to put on our show, and the big local hero this time was Rubens Barrichello. He and the Jordan team looked quite competitive. He was the great hope for all Brazilians, and he didn't disappoint them: he nearly got pole position. He went out in qualifying and, on his first run, was the quickest. He started on the front row of the grid ... alongside me. Unfortunately for him and his supporters I managed to nick pole and was delighted with the way we worked so well in qualifying. Adrian, Tim and the engineers set the car up perfectly and it was absolutely superb. We were eight-tenths clear of Rubens and there was no one between us. The next second covered twelve cars, so, on the face of it, I had a big advantage for the race.

But I knew that was no reason for complacency. I knew that if you feel you're in a comfortable position, that is the precise time when you should be worried, and should expect the unexpected. So, on Sunday morning, I was really committed and concentrating, and not at all surprised to discover that I was the crowd's public enemy number one. We did the parade lap on the back of a truck to the chant, from all the Brazilians, of 'Rubinho, Rubinho, Rubinho!' He was really pumped up, and there was no doubt that the Brazilians were there to support only one person. Then came the unexpected.

It was very hot all morning, with brilliant sunshine until about noon, when, suddenly, huge clouds appeared and soon emptied themselves of millions of gallons of water, just half an hour before the race was due to start. And when it rains in Brazil, it really *rains*. It just pummelled the whole place for thirty minutes and then, slowly, began to clear up. Normally, you can set your watch by the rainfall in São Paulo. It usually rains at about three o'clock, which is why the race starts earlier there than elsewhere, but someone had set the weather clock wrong this time: the rain came three hours early!

When it started, we'd been just about to leave the garage, but we had to change our plans completely. We'd decided that the best strategy for the race would be to go for two stops, but once it started raining like that, we had to go for a one-stop race. If it dried up, we thought, we could always switch back to a two-stop strategy, but that seemed pretty unlikely. On the grid, as I sat there in the car, I was very worried, because on the formation lap I'd seen where the water was draining off and backwashing up through the manhole covers at the side of the track. I knew that we were all taking a big risk racing in those conditions, because the car can aquaplane so easily.

A couple of years earlier there'd been a big shunt on the start–finish line, and loads of cars had gone off after losing control on the straight. I knew this, and I knew too that it was a potentially dangerous place because the straight is long and very fast past the pits towards the corner. There is no real escape, either, because there are high walls on both sides so you just cannot see what is coming until you're on top of it – and by then there's nowhere to go. All in all, the worst thing that can happen in Brazil is that you aquaplane on the start–finish straight – which is exactly the place where that sort of thing is most likely to happen.

I got on the radio to Patrick Head and told him I thought they should start the race with a safety car. All he and the team could do was listen to me, say they understood what I was saying and then have a word, but the team are not in control of the safety-car issue. Nothing happened on that score, so the race had to go ahead as normal. The rain abated a bit, but there was a lot of standing water. The key point at the start of a race like that is that, if you're behind someone, you can't see where you're going, so I knew I had to make sure I got ahead at the start. In those kind of circumstances, you are motivated by self-preservation to just get ahead, and you live on your wits, driving on a virgin track, one where none of the water has been dispersed because there are no cars ahead of you. You're just driving into the unknown.

When the lights changed, I made only an average start and I could see Rubens coming down the inside, so I had to block him to the left and that allowed Jacques to come around to the right, so I had to block him on the right at the bottom part of the first corner. Once I'd done that, I was in the clear, and my chief worry was how to judge my pace on a track as wet as that one. It was extremely difficult, but of course nothing like as difficult as it was for the people behind me. If you're at the back, more water has been dispersed, but it's dispersed into the air, making it difficult to see where you're going! Your vision is zero. I knew I'd got the edge by being in front, and I knew I had to make it count – and I did. I pulled out three or four seconds over the first lap, pushed on until I was about twelve seconds ahead and then eked it out to twenty. It was a bloody good lead and it gave me a tactical stranglehold on the race.

To make matters even better for me, our team strategy was just perfect. The weather broke and parts of the track began to dry out, but then it rained again. At some stages, it was raining heavily on the back part of the track, but completely dry on the start–finish straight. I knew the wet tyres would last no time at all on the dry track, because they overheat, the rubber melts, and you end up driving on little balls of rubber stuck to the tyre. So you have to seek out all the wet lines on the track to cool the tyres, and it was difficult, too, to try and judge when to change over. When we did finally decide to pit, about mid-way through the race, the weather was just about to turn and it was starting to ease off. It was just right. I got on to slicks and pulled out ten seconds in a few laps. The timing was perfect.

Of course, we had a little luck thrown in as well, which helped me to my eventual victory. But we really had everything to celebrate afterwards because, as a team, we'd worked it out perfectly, set it up perfectly and had dominated the event. Pelé, the best Brazilian footballer of the 1950s and '60s and one of the greatest sportsmen of all time, presented me with the trophy, and said it was a great honour to do so. I'd never met Pelé before, and I was truly honoured to receive it from him, Brazil's greatest hero and now their Minister of Sport. When you win, there are a lot of little things which come with the victory to make it special and memorable, and this was definitely one of them.

It was a great moment: a great win and a terrific result. But I was still mindful of how dangerous the conditions had been. At the start, driving towards that first corner, you are in a state of acute awareness that must be unique to this job. It is not mere nervousness: it is total awareness of all the sensations you're experiencing. You're driving by the seat of your pants. You feel the steering wheel, you feel every twitch, you feel the movement of the car underneath you. You end up kind of squeezing everything: you squeeze the throttle, the brakes, all of it. You don't do anything suddenly. And the whole thing is moving, sliding, and you're right on the edge. Suddenly it will break away and you have to catch it, but you don't act violently, you react quickly. It is almost as if the car is in touch with the road by its fingertips.

I love driving in the wet. It is one of the most wonderful experiences you can have, balancing the car in those conditions, because the car is able to slide more. In the dry, because of the way the tyres work, you can't actually drift that much. If it gets too out of shape, then the tyres lose their grip and you get too much oversteer. The tyres can't stand too much sliding anyway, because there's too much energy and they get hot and start to deteriorate, but in the wet they're designed to perform at that temperature. As long as it keeps raining, they'll

> **I love driving in the wet. It is one of the most wonderful experiences you can have.**

perform like that all day, and with the car sliding around it makes driving exciting and enjoyable.

Having said that, I won't go out and drive on a wet track for no reason. There is the added danger, the car will not decelerate as quickly as it does on a dry track, and if you spin off you don't lose any speed. The car will hit the barriers at the same speed you were doing when you left the track. In the dry, the car will spin, and on slicks it'll slow down an awful lot. Plus, in the wet, you can go off on the straight, so you have to concentrate three times harder because even the straights aren't safe – whereas in the dry you can tear down them flat-out to get to the next corner.

There are some times when a track is simply too wet to send racing cars out. In my view, that is why the safety car is there at Grands Prix. Those sort of conditions rarely persist for longer than half an hour and, afterwards, if you have got just a wet track, then most people can cope with it. Sometimes, too, wet races give drivers a real challenge. I had one at Suzuka in 1994, and in Brazil it was much the same. Jacques suffered because he had so little experience of racing in the wet (they don't race in the wet at all in IndyCars), but you couldn't say that for Michael Schumacher, Jean Alesi or Rubens Barrichello.

After winning that race, we celebrated and then I planned to go down to a place on the coast, which had been recommended to me by people who will remain nameless. The trip is about an hour and a half from São Paulo, and Georgie and I had a chauffeur to take us out of the city. It was Sunday evening, dark, and if you wound down the window you could hear the tree frogs and all the other myriad sounds of the jungle. We were looking forward to a few days off together before the next race in Argentina.

Unfortunately there was a bit of a mistake with our booking and, when we arrived, I must say the place didn't look that brilliant either. So we made an about-turn, jumped in the car, went back to the Hotel TransAmerica in São Paulo, met the team in the bar and ordered some more celebratory drinks. We had one ourselves, of course, and then bumped into Eddie Jordan. He suggested we went down to Rio with him to play some golf and relax, so we went along and it turned out to be a great three days. I stayed in the hotel mostly,

> **It was a great moment: a great win and a terrific result.**

lounging by the pool, but played a little golf and tennis and went boogie-boarding. The beach had some serious waves and everyone from the local area was surfing, including a few of the English press who I'd invited to use my board – half hoping it would make a story ('Hill saves *Sun* man from killer surf!'), but it didn't quite happen.

I had only one worry, which was when I was told that some 300,000 people lived in a *favela* nearby and that all their raw sewage flooded into that part of the sea. It gave me an attack of the cold sweats thinking I was going to go down with typhoid before reaching Buenos Aires … and, strangely enough, I did have a pretty bad tummy bug in Argentina. I don't know if it had anything to do with that beach, but it was nice to have been there, to relax and train and have Georgie with me. We don't have many opportunities like that. As ever it came to an end all too soon, and we flew down to Buenos Aires where, soon after arriving, I had a fairly serious brush with the local police.

I remembered, from my dad's stories about racing, that the police, particularly in places like Argentina, could be a little over-diligent, and it was worth giving them a bit of extra respect. One night during the run-up to the race I left the circuit – together with Jacques, his manager Craig

Pollock, my assistant Jamie McCallum and Jon Nicholson – to go to an oil depot owned by Elf for a promotional appearance. We did the usual thing: the pictures, the hand-shaking, the press conference and so on, and that was all fine. Then we were given directions back to central Buenos Aires, which we either misunderstood or didn't hear properly. We got lost. I ended up doing U-turns all the time, and we were getting nowhere. In the end, I did a U-turn at a dual carriageway intersection – right in front of a policeman. He blew his whistle and pulled me over.

I resisted saying, 'Oh, by the way, I'm Damon Hill, the Formula One driver – would you like my autograph?' but it soon became obvious that I might have to impress my VIP status on this guy. Unfortunately, he was having none of it and things began to look pretty serious. We were all contemplating a night in the Argentine dungeons, I think, working out ways of explaining what had happened. Jacques went very quiet. Jamie, who speaks some Spanish, tried to sweet-talk the policeman. I waved my official FIA pass at him and said, 'It's me, I'm terribly sorry … We've just come from the circuit and we're lost. Could you help us?' He simply hitched up his bullet belt, scratched his head and recited the rules. Then he told Jamie to go with him while we sat in the car.

He took Jamie off to a little hut and I was half tempted to step on it and leave Jamie there to sort it out, but after a few jokes about doing this we decided to wait. At least another ten or fifteen minutes passed, and we were getting quite anxious before Jamie re-emerged – with the policeman completely won over by something Jamie had said or done. He told us not to worry. 'Everything's okay now,' said Jamie, as he searched for an Elf T-shirt, which we signed. He gave the policeman the T-shirt and that was it. We drove away.

Only then, as we left this little episode behind us, did Jamie tell us that he'd paid the policeman $100, the usual 'unofficial' fine for a stop-and-go penalty, to let us go. We were just relieved to be free. We'd escaped an awkward-looking situation and, rather diplomatically, I made sure I avoided mentioning any of it when I met the President of Argentina, Carlos Menem, as I collected my pole position prize on Saturday afternoon …

The Buenos Aires circuit is small. It would be unkind to say it is a Mickey Mouse track, as it is twisty, tight and good fun to drive on, but it is a little on the small side for a Formula One car. Nevertheless, it does give us an opportunity to show what we can do. You can, for example, really slide it around, but you do have to be careful of the bumps. The previous year, the Grand Prix

Drivers' Association (GPDA) had made some suggestions to the organisers about removing the worst of the bumps, on the very quick right-hander on the back straight for instance, a flat-out sixth-gear corner with two very big bumps. But when we turned up we discovered they were still there – and worse than ever in their effect on the cars and their drivers. There was a lot of talk about these obstacles because they were starting to break the cars. There was even doubt about whether the circuit would be allowed to stage the race if the bumps weren't levelled out.

It was the usual sort of pre-race drama. But they got out their grinding machines and managed to improve things a little before the event started in earnest. At least we were able to get on with the job, and we had a very exciting qualifying session. I was fourth, with about three minutes to go, when I went out again and managed to get the car on pole position for the second successive race. It was quite the opposite to Brazil. There I managed to gain a big advantage on the first run, but in Argentina I needed to do two runs – and long ones, too, to try and generate some heat in the tyres. That's why I left my winning lap to the final minutes. It was still very difficult to get a clear run, as there were so many cars on the track, but I got the one I needed and Carlos Menem presented me with my trophy, the only prize of the year to mark pole position.

The Argentine fans are very seriously into Formula One. Carlos Reutemann attracted a lot of attention. A lot of Italians live there, too, along with a lot of Germans – and, of course, there was a German driving for Ferrari. It was understandable that there was a lot of support for the red cars. They only get one race a year, so they're really up for it and they make sure there is a good turn-out. They boo if you don't go out of the garage, and if something happens there's always a big cheer. They're a bit of a wild bunch, too, and the driving on the normal roads is something to behold. It's not that they lack lane discipline – they seem to lack lanes. On some of the motorways you can't even tell if it's a two-lane, three-lane or five-lane road. The Armco barriers we'd noticed the previous year, put there to prevent us from crossing the central reservation, were just laid gently on the grass this time. I'm not sure why – maybe they forgot, or maybe they never put them up properly in the first place. Either way, driving in Argentina is always interesting, and sometimes it seems to be safer on the track than off it!

The competition, on the track, was closer than before – and, to my discomfort and concern, I really wasn't feeling at all well. I started to suffer from severe diarrhoea on

Thursday. I'd never had anything like it in my life. I was up every two hours and didn't get much sleep at all. On top of this physical problem, there was a major domestic dispute in the hotel room next to mine at about four in the morning. I tried to get them to shut up, and actually ended up running along the corridors with Georgie and some security guards in an attempt to find out where all the noise was coming from. It was hardly a good night's rest to prepare for the race.

The following day I felt deprived of sleep; I'd not eaten much because of my stomach problems; and race day looked like it was going to be a scorcher. I knew it was going to be tough. It's a busy circuit for a driver, and we have to work quite hard to balance the car, so I had my doubts about lasting the distance. As we sat on the grid that was one of my major anxieties – quite apart from the fact that I had to go to the toilet again very shortly before the start of the race. I had to run there and back, and returned just in time.

This time I made a good start. I got ahead of Michael, and that was vitally important to me because, on that circuit, a slower car can hold you up for ever. But, from the front, I was able to dictate the race, and could pull away if I wanted to. I painstakingly built up a six-second lead when, as if to prove you can never count on anything in Formula One, the safety car came out because Luca Badoer's car had turned upside down. I had no idea what had happened, but assumed he'd got out of the car. The net result was that my hard-earned lead was slashed and Michael was sitting, threateningly close, on my tail.

In that situation, you just don't know how long you're going to be behind the safety car; you just go round and round at a snail's pace. Usually this would be a good opportunity to talk to the pits, except that on this occasion my radio had broken, so I had no direct communications from the team. I didn't realise it, but they could hear me quite clearly, but as I couldn't hear them at all the radio was as good as useless as far as I was concerned. It meant I was completely in the dark, so I had to work out how the race was going for myself and draw on my experience. I'd been the first driver in Formula One to lead a race behind a safety car, in Brazil

> **It meant I was completely in the dark, so I had to work out how the race was going for myself and draw on my own experience.**

in 1993, when it was wet, so I had some experience of the situation.

I told the pits I wanted them to use the pit-board to communicate with me, and just hoped they could hear. I would ask a question which could be answered 'yes' or 'no' – and I would see the answer when I passed by the pits two minutes later. My other problem was that the guy driving the Williams Clio safety car was hopeless. He was so slow I had to put the car in neutral most of the time. That's not a problem in itself, but if you drive an F1 car too slowly, the tyre temperatures go down, the pressures go down, and soon enough the car drops to the ground. I knew we were already pretty close to the limit, and we had these bumps on the back straight as well, so my biggest concern was whether or not the car would be off the deck enough when they decided to restart the race.

Eventually the guy in the pace car pulled off. I'd been anxious to get the exit from the last corner just right to avoid giving Michael an opportunity, but he dropped back at the hairpin to keep Jean Alesi back. Michael stamped on his brakes a bit in the middle of the last corner and wrong-footed Alesi. This stopped him from having a run at Michael going down to the first corner. Despite the safety car's interruption, this was exciting stuff, but in those first three or four laps after the restart, my car really smacked the ground when it went over the bumps. It carried on doing it until the tyre pressures came up again and the situation resolved itself. I was especially pleased to be through this phase as I was beginning to wonder if my back and teeth could take any more of this punishment. The impact on the bumps was so severe that my teeth and jaws were smashing together every time I went over them, and I could feel my lower back getting compressed violently each time. But I managed to drive on in front. The team made two fantastic pit-stops (the second was only about seven seconds) and I went on to win my second Argentinian Grand Prix.

As I stood on the podium they played the British national anthem. It was only a couple of days after they'd celebrated their Falklands (or Malvinas, I should say) remembrance services, and there was a lot of booing and hissing as 'God Save the Queen' was heard. It's not that

> **As I stood on the podium they played the British national anthem.**

long since the Falklands War, and I realised that relations remained somewhat strained.

But I knew too that I'd won my ten points, I'd secured my third win on the trot, and I'd made a perfect start to the season – so I wasn't going to let anything spoil my celebrations.

4 🏁 EUROPEAN & SAN MARINO

After the race in Argentina I felt pretty good – surprisingly good given the way I'd been feeling for the previous twenty-four hours. The race had taken an hour and fifty-five minutes, longer than Monaco, and I'd expected the worst. Credit for that was due, without any doubt, to Erwin Göllner for working round the clock to ensure I was in the best possible condition under the circumstances. I was amazed how well I felt and, of course, there was quite a celebration that night. With Jacques coming home second, it was a one-two for the team and this meant that Frank had to buy everyone dinner, a tradition we're all happy to maintain as often as possible!

It was only when I got home from South America and had a chance to watch a tape of the race on television that I realised how serious Pedro Diniz's fire had been. I was horrified. It was a real blaze. There hadn't been a lot of fuel, probably not much more than a gallon, which had caught alight, but it was clear that if his fuel leak had been combined with Luca Badoer's overturned car, it would have been a very, very dangerous situation.

This prospect, raised only a few weeks after Martin Brundle's crash in Australia, drew a lot of attention to the GPDA and the wider issues of safety in the sport. This is something I'm interested in, for obvious reasons. I know some people within the sport are suspicious about the GPDA, but I don't think they need to be. Drivers today are genuinely interested in avoiding problems, not in creating them. Everyone wants to get on with the racing and we all want our just rewards. But, of course, we want to do it in the safest possible way – and, preferably, through co-operation with the ruling body, the Fédération Internationale de l'Automobile (FIA). We know we can get things done that way. It's wrong for anyone to suspect that the GPDA wants control; that has never been on the agenda. We work, we co-operate and we communicate with the FIA to quite an impressive degree, but it is ironic that it took a great tragedy – Imola in 1994 – to make everyone grow up.

Formula One is a very political environment, and there's always something controversial happening or about to happen. For example, before the start of the season, the

GPDA had a dispute with the FIA over super-licences and the standing and status of the GPDA itself. Every year we are presented with a *fait accompli*, a contract called a licence application, which obliges us to do certain things and gets us to indemnify people from claims. Obviously this has insurance implications and causes quite a bit of unease among the drivers. There were a lot of arguments about this before the season began, and Max Mosley, the president of the FIA, said he didn't recognise the GPDA because they weren't a proper body. Something needed to be done so we had it registered in London, a decision announced in Argentina. It was more of a footnote to the Argentinian Grand Prix than anything else, but it was just another of those things that bubble away below the surface and occupy some of our time.

I feel it is impossible to ignore this sort of thing, and now the GPDA is a properly registered body I think it can play a role in improving safety standards in the sport. There is always going to be pressure on the drivers, too,

> **Formula One is a very political environment, and there's always something controversial happening or about to happen.**

from the establishment, to avoid being controversial, not to be negative about things, to help promote the image of the sport as a whole. That is inevitable, just as it is impossible not to be drawn into the political scene that surrounds those pressures. If you are not a high-profile driver, you can put your head down and ignore it, because you're just concentrating on hanging on in there. But the moment you become successful, and become one of the top half-dozen or so drivers, then you're a major part of the big picture, and often at the centre of any problems which arise. Drivers just cannot afford to sign away their rights, and that's why the GPDA took up a position and stood firm.

Some drivers have problems with insurance and with insurance companies, and we've looked at ways of helping them; some drivers have had injuries and are still waiting for their claims to come through. We hope we can really do something to help them because, as a group, the GPDA will have much more clout than any individual. I think we all have to retain our statutory rights, no matter what country we're in, and that's why the GPDA exists, why it matters and why we worked to set it up with all the necessary formal recognition.

All this was just a backdrop to the action in South America and, after flying home, I must say I enjoyed the sense of having really cleaned up. I felt ready for the European season and I was in a very positive frame of mind when we went down to Jerez, in southern Spain, to do some testing. It was our first test since the start of the season, and a good chance to do a few things we'd planned but hadn't had an opportunity to try. Jerez is also a similar track to the Nürburgring – the scene of the previous year's end-of-season disaster for me – and so I went there intent on working hard to make sure I had a much better time in Germany, at the European Grand Prix, than I'd had the previous year.

The test went well, I felt strong and I travelled to the Nürburgring full of optimism. There was no doubting I was on Michael Schumacher's home turf. The track is very close to his family home, and the supporters, who used to create a sea of Benetton blue around the circuit, were this time like an ocean of Ferrari red. The fans there are quite incredible. They've taken to Formula One with huge enthusiasm because of Michael, and, partly as a result of his success and popularity and partly because of our rivalry, I too have my share of German fans – even though it could hardly be said that I'm the most popular man in Germany!

After last year's result, I felt so much pressure to do well and to continue the form I'd shown in the first few races.

I knew everyone had had a chance to do some testing and it would be interesting to see how things shaped up. It was like a new beginning for us all. Our car was brilliant again and, after finding a good set-up, I was able to do one of my best-ever qualifying laps to claim pole position, seventenths of a second clear of Jacques. It was as clean a lap as I have ever driven, and it put everyone else in the shade. Many people were pointing to the improved horsepower of the Mercedes and Peugeot engines at this time, particularly in qualifying, and consequently I felt that my own qualifying performance was one of my very best. I think Michael was actually a bit shocked at the gap between him and us – but, quite naturally, I was really pleased.

Up to that time, Michael had been deflecting pressure from himself, and Ferrari, by down-playing his expectations. But, inside, I'm sure he believed he could win races with Ferrari. He'd shown competitive form in Argentina, and this was his home race, so he was bound to be disappointed at being adrift of the pace in qualifying, even though he was third quickest. I made sure I didn't get involved in any kind of propaganda with Michael, and simply concentrated on the job. Thankfully the weather was fine (like everyone else, I'd packed all my wet-weather gear in expectation of a repeat of the previous year's deluge), and that too made life easier.

Being on pole position, however, is worth nothing at all unless you make a good start. I'd made a dreadful start in Argentina, and should have learned from it, but I made another terrible getaway in Germany. Firstly I failed to get the clutch to bite properly, and then I had too much wheelspin. I dropped back four or five places. All the hard work of getting pole position, the beauty of that qualifying lap, was wasted. Quite understandably, after the race, we spent a long time looking very hard at the way we used the clutch.

David Coulthard was the one who did get off the line properly, making a storming start from sixth on the grid and almost leading the first lap. I was back in fifth, running in a pack of cars and frustrated at the knowledge that Jacques was out in front and getting away. It was to be a torrid race for me.

I managed to get past Michael on the start–finish straight, on lap six, sweeping past him right in front of the crowd, and then I started to make progress on Rubens. But I felt something strange with the handling, to the extent that I had to pit to get it checked out. It felt like the car had collapsed on the left front corner.

Needless to say the pit-stop cost me time, too much time, and put me down into the traffic. The reason for the handling problem was a mystery which we never solved:

the car was thoroughly examined after the race and found to be okay. In the light of the incident at the British Grand Prix, later in the season, a possible explanation was a loose wheel. As they all were changed at the pit-stop, as a matter of routine, the loose wheel problem would have been undetected at the end of the race.

One thing was certain, though: I'd not given up my position on the track lightly, but now had a near-impossible task to win. Points were my only realistic concern – as many of them as I could get my hands on before the finish. It wasn't easy, and I ran into more trouble when Pedro Diniz managed to nudge me and we both went off. I lost all the positions I'd fought for in the previous laps and fell back to tenth, but carried on thinking, 'I'm not coming all this way to get nothing' and just pressed on, and on, and on, until I managed to get up to fourth place by the end of the race.

Looking back I felt it was a race I could easily have won. I was quicker than anyone else on the circuit and, given that I'd overtaken Michael in the early part of the race and he'd finished a close second, I realised that without the handling problem I could have just sat behind Rubens for a long time and still won. But I did have a classic battle with David Coulthard over the last few laps, when he was trying every trick in the book to stop me getting past. He apologised afterwards, but he didn't need to: he hadn't done anything out of order at all except to take third place! I would have loved to have got on to that podium.

Afterwards I was a bit more objective, and actually felt it had been one of my best drives for a long time. I'd over-taken ten people in the race, I'd been very fast and had finished fourth. I knew the points would be extremely valuable later in the season. Unfortunately, not everyone shared my view. The press concluded that it was a disaster, that I'd lost my marbles and was cracking up, going to pieces. It was all doom and gloom. Luckily I'd learned my lesson from the previous year. I didn't read the papers and I managed to maintain my composure. There was only a week to the next race, at Imola, and I knew I needed a good result there.

I left Germany feeling it was a cursed place for me. In my first race there, at Hockenheim, I was leading Alain Prost by thirty seconds when I got a puncture on the last lap. Next time I crashed into Ukyo Katayama and had to have a long pit-stop which put me down half a lap, but I was half a second quicker than everyone else for the entire race. And last year I had a CV joint give up on the second lap, causing me to go off and crash despite having started from pole position. Germany has not been a good place for me – so I was quite glad to turn around, go home and then fly out to Italy.

If luck has never been with me in Germany, I felt it was never far away in Italy. I'd won at Monza twice and Imola once, and going into the San Marino Grand Prix I knew I had to put my championship campaign back on course. There were, of course, the difficulties posed by Ferrari, being on home turf, and by Jacques, boosted by his first victory, travelling to a circuit that he knew from testing. But I felt confident and determined.

As soon as you arrive at Imola you can feel the atmosphere: it's always Ferrari, Ferrari, Ferrari. The *tifosi* are very vocal in their support, and you're soon aware that you have extra competition, more than usual, from the red cars. It's a special kind of feeling, and it soon proved to be a reality in qualifying: they were quick straight away, and Michael was obviously pumped up to meet the massive expectations of the crowd.

It was his first Grand Prix in Italy since he'd joined Ferrari, and he had to do something special. He did it by bagging pole position, just managing to cross the line before his left rear wheel broke as he finished his final lap. He spun off and ended up in the gravel, as the session ended, but his luck was intact. I was second, and realised it was going to be a close race even if Ferrari were not going to be able to use their 'qualifying' engines, having to make do with less powerful versions, for the race itself.

It was Michael's first pole for Ferrari, and their first at Imola since 1983. The crowds were huge and very excited, even by Italian standards. They love their motor sport and their enthusiasm is infectious. I never felt any negative feelings at all and the reactions of the crowd towards me, as I went to and from the hotel, were always uplifting and encouraging.

I stayed at a hotel quite close to the town centre and the track. It wasn't a luxurious five-star affair, but it was very convenient. It is in a housing estate, and I stay there when I am testing at Imola too, so I'm used to it. It makes me feel I am living in an Italian community, because I can hear people's television sets, babies crying, kids playing in the street. It's a lovely atmosphere, and every time I returned to the hotel, the children from the area were out to get my autograph – along with just about everybody else's.

> **As soon as you arrive at Imola you can feel the atmosphere: it's always Ferrari, Ferrari, Ferrari.**

The only problem is that they pester the hell out of us all, because they always want more than one autograph and they're there every night. Even if I gave them one the night before, they come back for another the next day. But it does mean I can have some fun with them and tease them, and all that just makes the whole thing more enjoyable. They're able to love all the drivers, not just Ferrari, and they really show it. They say, 'You're the best – you're fantastic'; I reply, 'What about Ferrari?', and then they always come out with something like, 'No, not Ferrari, Damon Hill is the best and Williams is the best car …' You know damn well they'd say anything to get you to sign, but that's all part of their charm.

Unfortunately, charm or otherwise, I wanted to win the race and I knew I needed a tactic that would give me the opportunity to finish ahead of Michael. If we got away in grid order, with him leading and me second, it would immediately put the emphasis on pit-stops and strategy. I knew Ferrari would be taking a step back in performance, because they would be unable to race with the same powerful engines they used in qualifying, but I knew we had to outsmart them during the race as well. I put in a lot of extra effort on Saturday night, not just in setting up the car but also planning the strategy.

On Sunday morning, when I drove the car, it felt spot-on and filled me with confidence. I had a car that was well-balanced and we were right there in the warm-up. We'd decided to do a two-stop race. This wasn't unusual in itself, but we planned to do a very long first stint – so long, in fact, that it was very nearly half-way through the race. This was the tactic we'd devised to give us the edge, and while I was glad we were being adventurous and creative, I must admit I had a few anxieties about it.

After the warm-up, I went to the drivers' briefing and then on the drivers' parade lap. Going round the circuit, I could see then that there were enormous numbers of people already packed in. The banks everywhere were filled with Ferrari fans, but I got a good reception nevertheless. It was a truly invigorating atmosphere. I went back to the truck, into the morning debrief and then, when I was satisfied everything was okay, I went for a lie-down and a massage. It was while I was lying there, half an hour or so before we went out, that I started to think about the number of laps. I knew we were going to do a long stint, but to nearly half-way? I wasn't entirely certain we'd got it right.

Fifteen minutes before the pit-lane opened, I went back and told them they had to convince me on this one, because to go to nearly half-way through the race was a very long first run. We sat down and went through the whole thing again. Then team manager Dickie Stanford came and sat at the door and said: 'We've got to put the fuel in. What are you going to do? The car has got to go out.'

It's an unavoidable mathematical fact that the more fuel you put in, the slower you go. For every 10 kilos of fuel you load, the car will go a quarter of a second a lap slower. Roughly speaking, we use 150 kilos of fuel in the race, which means you have to juggle around with the weights and calculate their effects. Also, the more weight you put in the car, the more important the set-up becomes because the car behaves quite differently. And then there are the tyres. Are they going to get better (which is possible sometimes) or will they deteriorate? We add all these things up, but basically it comes down to whether I feel we've got the right balance or not. I took the decision to go for the long first run.

In previous seasons we'd been pretty conservative. Benetton were always known as the inventive team, but this time it was us doing something different. It was not a typical Williams tactic, by any stretch of the imagination, but I knew it would give me something in hand for the race. I wanted to be running my own race and I was pretty sure my competitors wouldn't be able to guess

The Melbourne track beckons: the start of the 1996 campaign.

Covered in oil, then in glory: coping with the results of Jacques Villeneuve's engine problem.

Away through the spray; en route to victory number two, in rainy Brazil.

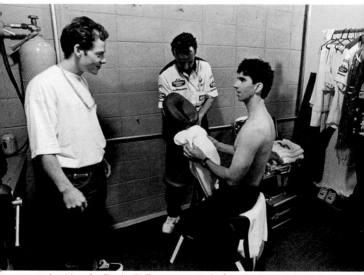

Awaiting the Erwin Göllner treatment before the Argentinian GP, with Jacques.

At the Nürburgring: enjoying the moment after clinching pole on Michael Schumacher's patch.

Tackling the Variante Alta (High Chicane) at Imola, during the San Marino GP.

The massed ranks of the Ferrari *tifosi* at Imola.

Lifestyles of the rich and famous: with Georgie during the run-up to Monaco.

'Hello, Jon!' Some of the corners are so tight at Monaco, you have time to take in a lot more detail than usual.

Monaco: the chicane on the harbour front. A victory seemed certain until my engine blew.

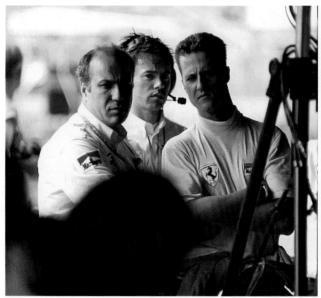
'What's he up to now?' Being checked out by the opposition in Spain.

'Well, guys, it's like this…' The media scrum at Magny-Cours.

Dickie Stanford (left) and James Robinson (right) line up for the British GP.

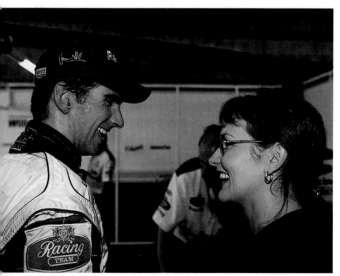

Georgie gives me something to smile about.

The pressure mounts during qualifying in Germany.

what the game-plan was. It was a key decision. It still gave us some flexibility, as we could change our plan during the race if we wanted to, but more importantly it also signalled the moment when we broke from our rather dull tactical traditions and became a bit more creative.

I got off to a good start. But David Coulthard, again, made a ridiculously good start and came from nowhere to lead. I was second, but I knew full well that I had a lot of fuel on board. I had to stay in touch with David and hold my own. If I could do that, I knew that things would turn out nicely. Jacques went out of the equation, but I had Michael crawling all over me and, one lap later, he got a good exit from the last corner and I could see him attacking down the inside. As we went into the next corner I thought about closing the door a little and leaving him to make his own arrangements, but it seemed an inappropriate time to be aggressive! He had

> **The plan worked beautifully: I never actually passed anyone, just drove the car, did nothing heroic and stuck to the programme, and it was a superb race for us.**

the advantage on the inside line, and I didn't really want to tangle with a Ferrari at Imola, not on that particular day. I didn't think I'd make it back to the paddock in one piece. Michael produced his 'Get out of jail free' card and I let him go off in pursuit of David.

This wasn't a particular worry, providing I kept pressing on and stayed within a certain distance. We had it worked out – I knew how many seconds I would be behind at a certain point in the race, and what sort of goals I had to achieve for myself. I knew things were going just about okay, and, of course, I pulled everything back when David and Michael went in for their first stops. I kept on going, and going, and going – until virtually half-way through the race, as planned. When they came back on to the track after their pit-stops, I'd passed them and was still on the circuit, on a lighter fuel load and therefore faster. When I was just behind them I was heavier, but after they'd stopped, they were heavier than me. The plan worked beautifully: I never actually passed anyone, just drove the car, did nothing heroic and stuck to the programme, and it was a superb race for us.

Michael's luck stayed with him, as it had in qualifying, by allowing him to complete the last lap with his wheel locked up after his suspension broke. That kept the *tifosi* happy. In fact, they were so happy they broke ranks and invaded the track, a transgression of the regulations for which Imola was later fined a cool one million dollars. It meant that about 130,000 people turned up at the prize-giving, at which I don't think I got a single cheer! But I was happy with the result, and the team had achieved an important goal by being strong in every area – tactics, performance, reliability and pit-stops. No one could accuse us of not being on the case for that race.

5 🏁 MONACO

I was due to stay on in Italy for more testing at Imola that week so, after winning the San Marino Grand Prix, I left the circuit late. There were still a lot of people around as I made my way back to the hotel, and one of them had obviously been waiting for me. He came up and thrust a paper bag through the car window, saying I had to have it. It was a bit of a surprise, naturally, and at first I thought he might be giving me his dirty laundry or something, because I'd beaten Michael in his Ferrari. I didn't really know what was going on … perhaps it was a bomb! But the guy obviously felt compelled to give me this bag, so I took it. When we got back to the hotel, I had a look inside.

It was amazing. Inside were individually-wrapped presents, complete with gift tags, for Oliver, Joshua, Tabatha, Georgie and myself, all done up beautifully in fine paper.

There were toys for the children and a piece of A4-sized paper on which my name was written hundreds of times, with each letter in a different coloured ink. It was incredible, and must have taken hours to do.

You only had to consider the chances of this bloke going to the track, carrying his bag of presents all day – including the piece of paper, which I think one of his kids must have given him – and then finding me and actually giving it to me. He didn't have a paddock pass, because he was outside the circuit, so the chances of him finding me in that massive crowd were pretty remote. It was a very touching act, typical of Italy. They're so whole-hearted in their attitudes and I must say I felt quite humbled, and moved – particularly at the end of such a satisfying and special day.

The next morning we were back to work: three days of testing, pounding round Imola again and again. I don't want to complain, but after the race weekend and then the testing I was more than a little pleased to get home. I needed a week's rest, some time to wind down and prepare for the next race, one that everyone always recognised as special: Monaco.

It was a prospect I relished. I felt that Imola had stunned a few people. They were used to seeing the Williams team doing things in a certain way, but our performance there had served notice that we were capable of doing things quite differently and wrong-footing people. It was the way Formula One has to be played and we'd proved we could do it.

My contention had always been that Williams was an engineering firm that went racing, rather than a racing team who engineered a very good car; but that victory proved that all the work we'd done in the winter, to create a team that operated as a racing, tactical arm to the engineering operation, had succeeded. Everyone in the team could draw satisfaction from Imola, and I was delighted to have answered those critics who'd reacted like headless chickens after the previous race and said I was cracking under pressure. I think we'd answered our critics in more ways than one, and done it quite forcibly, so we were feeling pretty confident as we gathered in Monte Carlo.

The Monaco race is a one-off. It is different to the rest

> **My contention has always been that Williams was an engineering firm that went racing, rather than a racing team who engineered a very good car.**

of the season. It is the only race in the calendar which gets such massive publicity worldwide, more than any other except perhaps the opening event or the one where the world championship is decided. It is right up there along-side the Indianapolis 500 and the Le Mans 24-hour race as one of the three biggest and most famous races in the world.

It also coincides with the Cannes Film Festival, so it has a glitzy image and attracts a lot of people who like to be seen and photographed in the paddock or the pit-lane, which is one of the most inappropriate pit-lanes for Formula One. Somehow, we all cope. People almost trip over themselves, we have tiny little boxes in which to pack our computers and tools, no one can move comfortably and it's just generally exhausting. But it's Monaco – and there's simply nowhere else like it.

This year the paddock appeared to be completely uncontrolled. People seemed to wander in and out as they pleased, which meant all the drivers were fair game for autograph-hunters and fans. This made life even more difficult. I'd never want to keep the fans away from me, but when I'm trying to work, to prepare for the race, it just adds to the problems. Simply getting from the motor-home to the pit-lane meant having to run very fast and finding all sorts of different routes to avoid being stopped and bogged down. If I didn't adopt these kind of tactics, I'd never get to the pit-lane on time! This kind of thing, plus all the extra media attention, the additional day (we arrive on Wednesday, practise on Thursday, have Friday off and qualify on Saturday), and the sheer logistical problems of moving around in Monte Carlo make it a very demanding weekend.

It is a daunting challenge. Much is made of the fact that my father won there five times, that he was synonymous with the place in the 1960s and that, until Ayrton won six Monaco Grands Prix, it was 'his' circuit, but none of that means anything extra to me – I simply want to win there because of the unique nature of the circuit and the event.

In terms of the track itself as well, Monaco is a one-off. Our cars aren't designed to drive round places like Monte Carlo. They're designed for places like Silverstone, or Estoril, or the Nürburgring, where there are longer corners and higher speeds and where the aerodynamics work properly and the suspension is more appropriate. If we were only going to race at Monaco, or somewhere like it, on a regular basis, we would build a completely different kind of car. But, instead, we go there with a compromise set-up and things on the car that we would never normally run anywhere else.

The premium is always on making the best possible use of the time. There is very little time available and the track, because it is a street circuit, is not very clean at the start, but becomes grippier as more and more rubber goes down during the weekend. This means that it offers the most grip in the final minutes of the qualifying session. Getting the car right at Monaco is like hitting a moving target, because you can never be sure if your improved times are due to the grip or to changes made to the set-up.

You can never be sure you're doing the right thing. This year was my fourth time at Monaco, but it was Jacques' first, and he had the added difficulty of still learning about a Formula One car. After his first run I asked him what he thought of it – and he said it seemed a lot smaller in an F1 car. That is precisely what I felt and I understood exactly what he meant.

When you get in the car at Monaco and drive round that track, you get a true feeling of claustrophobia. There's nowhere to move, there's hardly enough space for the car; it's an amazing feeling – and yet it's also one of the most satisfying places you can ever drive, precisely because of these reasons. There is nowhere to rest, the driver is always having to second-guess the car and anticipate everything. I look at black marks on the track, which indicate rubber, and scuff marks on the kerbs and I know these are places that can be used. If there are no marks, it probably means there will be some dust and no one wants dust on their tyres because it could mean sliding off.

And then there's the tunnel – usually I just hold my breath and hope, because I can't see round the corner – and if the track is blocked, there's nowhere to go. There was a close call in qualifying this year, when Gerhard Berger came through and found Michael there in front of him waving to the crowds after his pole position lap! Understandably Gerhard wasn't best pleased.

Monaco is just an awesome place to drive around. We race at waist height and, because of that, there are some odd things that a driver can see from his car. Parts of the circuit are very slow and don't have any barriers. When people are standing there, taking pictures or spectating, you can see them clearly. At some places, a lot of photographers will congregate and hang over the barriers and I've found I can see their faces and actually recognise them, even while I'm driving the car. For example, on one lap this year I was going round Loews hairpin and caught sight of a girl there, taking a picture. She was wearing quite a short skirt and was kneeling down on one knee, and I could see a lot more than I think she intended me to! When I told Georgie and Jon Nicholson about this later, they didn't believe me – didn't believe I had time to take in details like that – so I told Jon I'd wave to him when I saw him the following morning.

The next day I went out on the track, saw Jon and gave him a wave – and he thought it was hysterical. It may sound amazing that a driver can be aware of so much other than just the track, but I believe the experience is all to do with concentration. When I'm driving the car my mind is taking everything in, every little thing. It is wide open, looking for all the things it needs to know and to recognise; it is completely impressionable and doesn't really miss anything.

Another aspect of Monaco's uniqueness is the tightness of the track, hemmed in by barriers for large parts of the circuit. I've always felt more comfortable with steel barriers than concrete ones, but, in all honesty, it probably makes very little difference. It's better not to hit anything at all, if you can help it. But at Monaco it's almost inevitable that you're going to hit the barriers from time to time.

Up to qualifying and the race, I'd touched them three times, just glancing blows. I carried on, because they weren't major and because such impacts are just part of finding those extra tenths to shave off the lap time. The car can stand a little bit of nudging, but if I was to go another five millimetres closer to the barriers, it could mean the suspension goes or even a wheel taken off. These possibilities do tend to force you to concentrate even harder, and the result is that you feel very intense, completely locked into the job. And that, of course, is the buzz. It is total concentration.

Monaco comes in for a lot of criticism because of its apparent disregard for modern safety standards. The argument goes that if it was a new venue for a Grand Prix then we'd never consider racing there. I think there's a lot of truth in that, but it doesn't allow for its unique sense of history. I think we'll be going there for a good few years yet.

I've been a spectator at Monte Carlo and I know there's nowhere to match it, anywhere in the world, to watch Grand Prix cars in action and to be impressed by their sheer power and speed. There are places at Monaco which make your hair stand on end. For example, if you watch from inside the swimming pool complex, you can feel the vibrations physically come through your chest; and if you walk through the tunnel – well, that's another world. In the army they teach you to open your mouth if there are shells going off, because otherwise you can get a shock to the chest and it can damage you internally. Going through the tunnel at Monaco has a similar effect.

There's a sudden compression of air with the car rushing into that confined space. It's like driving a plunger down a tube.

And all around, the sound is bouncing off the buildings. Communication is virtually impossible and the combination of the concentration, the noise and the sheer effort of it all takes its toll mentally. By the time I get back to the hotel I'm completely bombed, drained of everything. When you leave the paddock, there are the fans and the autograph-hunters trying to get you. One of my nicest experiences at Monaco, therefore, is getting back to my hotel room and shutting the door! I still love it, though. I complain all the time when it's happening, but I know it wouldn't be the same if it was done any other way.

This year we were under pressure in qualifying, and I knew I had a fight on my hands. It is, obviously, very important to get on the front row because overtaking is nigh-on impossible. Pole position is a huge advantage, and I wanted to follow up the result at Imola with another demonstration of my and Williams' ability. Everything went well and I was very satisfied with the preparations, but when it came to qualifying I didn't really get a good run-in on my first couple of laps.

I wasn't able to get the last part right on the first two

runs. This meant I was languishing in fourth place and needed a good, clear lap if I was to secure a good position on the grid with my final effort. I pushed as hard as I could and moved, provisionally, into pole position – but in my heart I knew I'd gone too early. The track was still improving and Michael and Gerhard had opted to go later, after me. Predictably, Michael pulled one out and took pole and, momentarily, forgot that Gerhard was still on the track and on his quickest lap too. It was then that the waving incident happened, forcing Gerhard to spin, which may have saved my front row position. It's not often that Michael does me that kind of favour!

Pole position at Monaco is the place to be. Second is all right, but anything further back and you're reduced to hoping for something miraculous to happen if you have designs on winning. I was second, and I knew that the race would almost certainly, as always, be between the two guys on the front row – me and Michael. The guys behind were looking for their 100–1 chances to pay off.

I don't know exactly why, but I had a feeling that Michael was just a little too confident about his pole position and his prospects for the race. Ferrari's success had helped to swell the crowds, he was certainly up for it and their performance was good. But there was something I sensed which gave me a little extra competitive edge as I began preparing on Saturday evening. It was still with me when I woke up on Sunday, and then something else happened: it rained.

Wet weather around Monaco isn't so bad, unless it rains very hard. Then it becomes truly hazardous, and also extends the race time. Two hundred miles is a long enough race as it is for that circuit, so rain just adds to the difficulties. It is a one-stop race, tactically, because overtaking is so difficult.

If you made more stops you'd never get through the traffic and recover the time. All these thoughts were in my mind as I considered the wet weather and the race. I reflected on how Michael had seemed just a bit too confident; he may have thought, after winning pole position, that the race would be a formality. I knew this could be a flaw. I knew that if I made a peach of a start, I had a great chance – especially in the wet. It would have been much more difficult to pass him on the run to the first corner in the dry. The rain had played into my hands by making the job of starting less predictable.

> **I knew that if I made a peach of a start, I had a great chance – especially in the wet.**

I hardly got any wheelspin at all, but Michael did and the rest all happened instinctively. The moment I saw his rear wheels spinning, I knew it was my chance. When you've been driving for a while, your mind is tuned into everything, including passing other cars, and I knew this was my chance – then, right at the start.

I knew it might be another thirty laps before another opportunity arose, and in those conditions it was like a gift from heaven. In the back of my mind, I always find room for thoughts about the other drivers, the opposition; it is all part of the big equation of race preparation. I had a sense that he just didn't expect me to go past him. I was aware of this, but didn't let it disturb my concentration and I just went for it. I went past him, focused completely on the next corner and pressed on. Then, just before the tight bend leading into Mirabeau, I looked in my mirror and wondered where Michael was. He was there, but just a little further back than I expected.

The corners come thick and fast at Monaco and I didn't know what the gap was. I couldn't see him. I just kept getting +4, +8 and then +12, and I remembered thinking nine seconds ahead in three laps was just beautiful. By then I didn't have a clue what was going on behind me, and I had no real idea of what had happened to Michael until later in the race, when I got a signal to tell me he was out.

After the race, people asked me what I thought when Michael went out, but I couldn't give them an answer because at the time I was loving every second of the race, and feeling I was on top of everything. The concentration required is so intense, a total discipline. Our strategy was to use as much fuel as possible to get us deep into the race and provide a big window for the weather. It worked perfectly. The dry weather came within three laps of my stop so, when I switched over to slicks, after twenty-eight laps, it was great timing and I was able to pull out a lead on Jean Alesi of something like six seconds in one lap.

The gap to Alesi, at that stage, was my only concern. A drying track is not easy, particularly at Monaco. This is because the surface is cool, because of the rain, and there are only narrow lines on the circuit which can be used. This means the tyre temperatures go down and they don't work as they are designed to, through lack of heat. It is quite tricky. All this was in my mind as I pressed on until lap forty-one, when a red light came on in the cockpit. My heart sank. It was a warning light. I got on the radio to ask what was happening, but before they had time to respond I went into the tunnel and discovered the answer. The engine self-destructed, a plug came out and oil went everywhere, nearly causing me to spin into the barriers. To my bitter disappointment, after doing everything I could, my Monaco Grand Prix was over. It was just rotten luck. A rare, very rare, Renault mistake had ended my race.

Williams hadn't won at Monaco since 1981, and the team's disappointment was just as big as mine. We'd thought it might be my first win there, and their first in fifteen years. But all those thoughts, those dreams, went up in smoke. I had a long walk back to the paddock, but I received a tremendous reception from the crowd as I went.

That was nice, of course, but there's nothing worse than hearing a race you should be participating in continuing without you in the background. I watched the rest of it, but had no feelings either way about the result. I wanted only to forget all about it, to get on with the next one. The fact that Olivier Panis drove brilliantly to give Ligier their first win since 1981 meant nothing, although the fact that Jean, Michael and Jacques all dropped out would have a bearing on my championship.

When I got back, Frank said, 'Fantastic drive, Damon.' I could only reply by saying that he didn't seem to have much luck in Monaco. Before the weekend, someone had given him a silver dollar and, for luck, after the race, he decided to give it to Joshua, who had been with us for the weekend. Josh played with it on the floor and then left it lying around, so I picked it up and put it into my briefcase. I thought it seemed quite a nice thing and, being a bit of a magpie, I kept it. I wanted, also, to have a change of fortune for the next race in Spain — and I hoped this dollar would do the trick.

❝ ... there's nothing worse than hearing a race you should be participating in continuing without you in the background. ❞

6 🏁 SPAIN

Renault were as sorry about Monaco as I was. They apologised profusely, and I vowed to come back next year and try again. After that, as far as I was concerned, it was all over and done with. I moved on, and began thinking about Barcelona, a track I had down on my list of favourite circuits. It has fast corners, which I felt would be good for our car, and the Williams team had a good record there – although, in retrospect, I should have realised that this never bodes well for me! I thought it would be a place where I could get a perfect balance, and just thinking about it lifted my spirits after the disappointment of Monaco.

Only two days later, however, we were back to testing at Silverstone. It was a rude reminder that this job is not all about glamour or glitz, but mostly about the hard grind of working to prepare and perfect our cars to win

Grands Prix. When the Silverstone test was over, I was pleased to get home to recharge the batteries. Driving six days out of seven can dull the appetite for speed a little.

It was the time of year when the pressure begins to build: the races are coming thick and fast and there is little chance to break the tension. It can be tiring, and this is where your pre-season training really pays off. All the extra hassle of going to airports, waiting for delayed planes and carrying luggage can take its toll. For this reason, I took the bold and expensive step of hiring a private jet. It may sound like a luxury, but the reality is that a lot of private airfields are much closer to the circuits we go to than the international commercial ones. They pose less problems for check-in and enable you to move quickly on towards your destination. It meant, also, that I could relax and think about things a little, instead of feeling besieged. I'd been with Frank Williams in the company jet from Oxford before, and that had made life a lot easier, allowing me much more time, so I knew what to expect. Now I could fly directly from Dublin to all the events, do the race and be home in time to see the news. Not bad!

After Monaco, Barcelona's paddock is a breath of fresh air. It is big, wide open and pretty uncrowded. There is less sense of claustrophobia, and on the whole it's a good, modern facility. As usual, I met the press on Thursday afternoon. We talked about my misfortune in Monte Carlo, and I stressed how keen I was to rebound from it immediately. I felt that with ten races to go we were coming in to the crunch part of the season, and that the next five races would be vitally important. I wanted to help encourage the team to focus on each race as competitively as possible, and I threw in a few observations about the apparent strength of the opposition, who it seemed were improving all the time. I also made a few remarks about the cars' power, and suggested that it was time Renault dug in a bit and found something to consolidate their performance edge.

The next day, in practice, Eddie Irvine was quickest in his Ferrari. It didn't mean a lot because, with the elimination of provisional qualifying sessions, Fridays had become nothing more than what I call 'fun days', and the times were not significant. It is just a day to set up the car and practice, but, like everyone else, of course, we want to be as competitive as we can. We don't always run to our maximum potential on Friday, but occasionally we do, and that has an effect on our times. So, because everyone plays their cards close to their chests, Fridays have become a low-key spectacle, and in Spain, where motor racing is left behind by football and bull-fighting in terms of popularity, the atmosphere is fairly low-key anyway.

There's none of the passion of Italy or Germany for example, and, as a result, the Friday in Barcelona was one of those days which passed by without much incident at all. Almost like a test day.

Things were a bit more interesting on Saturday. To start with, Renault had invited David Ginola, the Newcastle United and France footballer (and model and sex symbol), as a guest, and that gave me an opportunity to tease Georgie a little when I called home. She's not an avid follower of football, by any means, but somehow she happened to have heard of Ginola. I think she saw a picture of him with no shirt on once, which must have made some sort of impression ...

In qualifying, I managed to find the perfect set-up, and I was four-tenths of a second quicker than Jacques, which was a good margin considering he'd tested intensively at Barcelona. He was keen to recover after Monaco, where he'd had very little luck, but an engine failure in qualifying did little to assist him. I had a couple of problems with punctures, too, but for Jacques it was a more serious problem and, after seeing a couple of other faults with the engines, the press decided it was time to ask a few questions about Renault. I said I wasn't too happy with the situation, pointing out that while Renault continued to supply their famed reliability, the need for horsepower to go with it was becoming quite urgent. I explained at the time that we were all working together to achieve our aim, which was a reliable, high-performing and competitive engine. I felt we needed to do something fairly soon, because there were other engines which were drawing closer and closer on power.

My comments obviously aroused some interest, and quite a few people joined in with their views. However, Renault, unbeknown to me and nearly everyone else in the paddock, were considering rather weightier matters: their whole future in Formula One, in fact. It was a delicate time, because of that, and it seemed I'd expressed my views without too much delicacy!

Unfortunately, on Sunday morning, it was wet. At first, this was not a great worry: I'd gone to Spain with high hopes, and these were raised even more after the warm-up because I was a second quicker than the nearest

> **The car felt very good, very competitive, and I was happy with things and confident that there was no need for me to change anything. But then the weather turned.**

guy. The car felt very good, very competitive, and I was happy with things and confident that there was no need for me to change anything. But then the weather turned.

The warm-up session had been stopped early because Heinz-Harald Frentzen had a huge crash into the pit-wall. He came out of the last corner and crossed the track into what appeared to be the pit-wall, but was actually a steel access gate. It was a sliding gate on rails, but it wasn't held in place properly and Frentzen hit it so hard it jumped off the rails, broke the catches designed to hold it in position and forced it to fly open into the pit-lane. At the same time, he spread the rest of his car all over the track.

They had to stop the session. Mercifully, Heinz-Harald was okay, but it could have been a very nasty accident. It brought home to me again that no matter how good you think a circuit is, in terms of safety, there are always things which can become unforeseen hazards. The net result, apart from the destruction of his car, was that it was impossible for me to go out again in those final minutes when the weather deteriorated further. The rain really started to pour down. The track had been wet when I set my time in the first fifteen minutes of the session, but nothing like as wet as it was at the end – or as it was going to be in the afternoon.

This, of course, had a direct bearing on the race, since the set-up I used was based on it being dry. It felt very finely balanced, and felt great. But, later, as I went out on the warm-up laps before the formation of the grid, I realised things were much worse than we'd expected: it was seriously wet, and I realised I needed to do something to change the set-up on my car.

We decided to go for more of a wet-weather set-up, but it turned out that we didn't go far enough. I'd been put off making more of a drastic change by the fact that the car was very quick in the warm-up – so quick, in fact, that I didn't want to interfere too much.

On the grid, however, it became plain that the weather and the track conditions were perilous. There was talk of the safety car being deployed. This had been discussed at Monaco the previous week, and the regulations had been changed to allow the first few laps of a race to be run behind a safety car. While I was on the grid, I told the team that I thought the race should start with a safety car because the conditions were so bad. While it would have been quite good for me if I'd got off the line first, in those conditions, the people in the middle of the grid wouldn't be able to see anything. It would be a big gamble to go ahead. Then, at the three-minutes-to-go signal, we got the message that the start would be as normal.

As a driver, I knew that the only thing to do was to think ahead. Once you get in the car, your mind is in a committed state. You have to think forward, be positive and decide how you're going to cope with any kind of situation. It is impossible to start arguing the toss about how the race is going to be run. There is no time for that. You simply have to start thinking ahead and concentrating.

I couldn't have guessed that the additional rain which fell between the warm-up and the start of the race would have made so much difference, but the conditions were appalling. I pride myself on being able to drive in all conditions, and after Suzuka in 1994, when they could only be described as atrocious, I felt that I could cope with anything. But no sooner had the lights changed than Jacques had beaten me into the first corner and I'd slipped back behind Jean Alesi. I soon realised I was in big trouble.

I made a bad start, and consequently lost the biggest advantage you can have in the wet: vision. It was almost

We have red lights on the back of the cars, but you can't see them in conditions like those: it was a total white-out.

113

impossible to see, and as I came down the start–finish straight on the first lap, there was – unbeknown to me – an accident further ahead down the straight. As I was ploughing through Alesi's spray, at about 180mph, I suddenly noticed, with no more than fifty yards' warning, that four or five marshals were working on two cars on the left. I also saw a Marlboro car on the right. It was impossible to see them until I was there. If the track had been blocked, there was no way I would have known. We have red lights on the back of the cars, but you can't see them in conditions like those: it was a total white-out.

The rain just kept pouring down. I had problems staying on the track on the straight, and I spun. I just couldn't get the balance I'd enjoyed in the morning and the car just wanted to step out on me every time I braked. I ended up going in the gravel on lap four, but made it back on to the track. I knew I'd lost a lot of positions, but I carried on. Then I went off again at the end of the back straight on lap eight. By then I was wondering if I could keep this going for a whole race. But before I'd worked out an answer, or formulated any kind of plan, I lost it in the last corner and was heading towards the wall, at exactly the same spot that Heinz-Harald had had his big accident in the morning. I braced myself for a big impact, but mercifully the car spun round a little more than H-H's and I took just a glancing blow. It was still enough to break the suspension, though.

I remember jumping out and thinking, 'Thank God that's over.' While I would never throw in the towel, I knew it was unlikely that I would have got much further in that race. I'd felt, while I was driving, that it was pretty likely I'd go off at some point, and so when it happened I was just grateful not to have been hurt. It was a race I had to put down to personal miscalculation of conditions. If I could go back and do it again, I know exactly what I'd do now, but the truth was that I made a crucial error in overlooking and underestimating how much the conditions had deteriorated during the day. I'd gone for a half set-up rather than a full wet set-up, like the one Michael Schumacher had on his car. He went on to win the race by quite a distance, and I was left kicking myself. If I'd chosen correctly, I think Michael and I would have had a classic tussle for the lead. I have no doubt that I would have beaten him in the dry, and I believe I could have won in the wet, too, if I'd got the set-up right. Unlike Monaco, Barcelona was a race where I dropped the ball myself, and it was a pretty unhappy trip home, despite the convenience of private jet travel. I knew what I'd done wrong, but I knew I had to learn from the experience and put it behind me.

I was also painfully aware that I'd failed to finish the last two Grands Prix, and that the gap between myself, Michael and Jacques had closed dramatically. I had to focus on doing well again in the next race and opening that gap up again. It was clear that this championship was not going to be plain sailing.

> " I had to focus on doing well again in the next race and opening that gap up again. It was clear that this championship was not going to be plain sailing. "

7 🏁 CANADA & FRANCE

The silver dollar I'd kept after Monaco went into a box at Heathrow on my way out to Canada. After two bad races, it was bringing me nothing but bad luck, so I ditched it and vowed to reject all superstition in future. Luck is a relative concept anyway.

Montreal is a fun place, the focal point for all Formula One fans in North America, and a city I think everyone enjoys visiting. I've been there a few times now, and I know it well enough to always relish the trip, so it gave me something bright to look forward to after Spain.

This year, on the way out, I decided to drop in on New York with a friend. I spent thirty-six hours there, going out one night and then spending the whole of the next day doing the New York experience in cabs, where the drivers can only be likened to kamikaze pilots on drugs. It was great fun, and a bit of an eye-opener for me, too, because no one gave a damn about who or what I was. It had been a long time since I'd been out on the streets, in shops or restaurants, and nobody had paid me any attention at all. To be honest, I'm not sure I liked it!

After this brief foray into the Big Apple, we hopped on to a plane for the hour's journey up to Montreal. After two non-finishes, I knew I had to do something in this race or the results would become a burden. So, when I arrived, my line for the media was that I wanted to finish the race, above all else, and that I couldn't afford to drop any more points. That, of course, was my public speech. Inside, I knew that the only place I wanted to finish was first. I knew that once you start to concentrate on just finishing a Grand Prix, you are haunted by the prospect that you may not. My goal was to win, not least because this was Jacques' home race. I knew that if there was anywhere he wanted to do anything, to come anywhere close to me, this was the place. It was sure to be his best shot up to that time.

He was on home soil, extra-motivated and he knew he could close the gap. I realised that he and Michael were my realistic title rivals, and I knew that Jacques was familiar with the track from his Formula Atlantic days. I knew, too, that he would be tough to beat – but also that, if I could win, it would be an enormous psychological bonus.

The circuit in Montreal is very close to the city centre, with a great atmosphere and a beautiful climate. Everywhere I went I got a good reception, and there was a tremendous amount of interest in the race. The restaurants were all full of race fans, from all over the United States and Canada. Obviously all the Quebec people were rooting for Jacques, but they were very polite and supportive towards me, and that was impressive. I met people from Alabama, Texas, Ohio and Idaho, all there in Montreal for the Grand Prix. They seemed to know a lot about Grand Prix racing too, and I think it's a real shame there's no race in the States.

They were nearly all Jacques fans. But they were also motor racing fans. They were very good at coming up and wishing me well, hoping I would win the race and demonstrating a typically American positive mental attitude. The once-a-year factor helped to make the atmosphere special, I am sure, for everyone. We went out on Saturday evening to an Italian restaurant where,

> **In some ways, it was a good thing for me that there was so much pressure on Jacques. The local media were all over him.**

naturally enough, all the waiters were decked out in Ferrari kit and the owner was wearing a Ferrari cap. When I arrived though, he managed to rustle up a Rothmans Williams Renault cap, and changed his allegiance for the night. Only Italians can do this!

In some ways, it was a good thing for me that there was so much pressure on Jacques. The local media were all over him. They called it Jacques-o-mania, and they wanted as much from him as they could get. He must have felt it, because on Thursday he was nowhere to be seen. He'd obviously decided to lay low and keep out of the spotlight as much as possible. Everywhere he went he was hounded. He also had some extra pressure from his father's brother, Uncle Jacques, who had gone to the press and said some rather unkind things about him. It was turning into a bit of a traumatic weekend for him, even before the race started, and I got the impression he was looking forward to returning to Europe.

I knew how he was feeling, because I've been through it myself at the British Grand Prix. The local boys are the centre of attention at home, and in Jacques' case it was even worse because he's about the only successful Formula One driver Canada have had since his father. It was easy to understand all the excitement, and easy to see the effect it was having on Jacques.

I think he'd pumped himself up to really perform to his best in Canada. In those kind of circumstances, you can feel relieved to get into the car and into action, but you also draw energy from all the hype. He was quick, very quick. I had a job on in qualifying to deal with him, and we were very close right through the weekend. But in the end, I managed to pull it off, even if it was only by half a second. That didn't bother me. Even if it's only one-thousandth of a second it is enough. I had pole position and had struck the first psychological blow.

One of the unusual things about qualifying in Canada is the way the tyres work. It is best to do two long runs, staying out on one set of tyres for as long as possible, because they produce their best time on the fourth lap. That means you can only do two runs to stay inside the qualifying limit of twelve in all. In an hour's session, it would be possible to have the whole thing over with in twenty minutes, but it doesn't work like that. Everyone waits because the track gets cleaner and quicker, and that means there is a kind of Mexican standoff while everyone waits for someone else to go out first.

While all this was going on, I was waiting by my car. I knew it would be a late start, so I just wandered around in the garage and I noticed, as I nipped around the back, that instead of the monitors all showing squiggly lines from the computers, they were showing Paul Gascoigne scoring a goal for England in the European Championship football match against Scotland. He kept on scoring that goal, over and over again. The match had been over for hours, but someone at the Williams factory had taped it and then modemed it to the garage in Montreal, where the guys had it on a repeat loop. Every time the ball hit the back of the net, the footage returned to the start of the move, with Gazza lobbing the Scottish defender and then volleying home. I don't know that much about football, but it looked a pretty good goal to me. So, while qualifying was going on all around us, most of the team were watching the football at the back of the garage. It certainly relieved the tension – and helped inspire me.

I was determined not to let the pressure get to me at all. I've learned a few things about myself in the last few years, and I've applied the knowledge regularly this year. I like to stay relaxed and withdraw into myself a little, trying to find that crucial bit of inspiration for the race ahead. I believe the England rugby team watch a film or something before a game – I know it's only a small ingredient, but all these things help in preparation, and I think in some strange way that Gascoigne's goal helped me get pole position that day.

This was an important pole to capture. Jacques had said, when he arrived, that he wasn't going to play the number two role. He was there to prove a point. I knew what this meant. Furthermore, at Williams, there are no team orders. They simply do not operate with them, or very rarely do, so I knew what to expect. They have a philosophy that they provide the machinery and the drivers are then left to do the rest. This is all very well when the team is fighting another team, which in this case was Ferrari, and I knew that there was no point in thinking otherwise. The question of Jacques being asked to come second never entered the equation. He was in Canada; a win was expected of him. And, through all this, he maintained a very good relationship with me. He was always confident, but he never seemed to let it become personal.

I think he was a little bit disappointed in his performance after qualifying. I think he felt he could have gone a little quicker on the last run than he did, but I felt sure he'd pick himself up and be just as quick and determined as ever for the race. The pressure, then, was on me. He'd closed the gap in Spain, and I faced a double threat, in Montreal, from him and from suffering another nonfinish. I simply had to get my head down and show everyone what I was made of again, on a circuit where, in the past, I'd not had much success.

This time, they had changed the circuit back to the format it was in when I first went there. This meant that from the hairpin back to the last corner, the chicane and the pits was a long straight again. In turn, this meant we ran less downforce on the car than in previous years, a strategy that Ferrari for some reason did not follow. As a result, Michael was quicker on the first part of the lap, but would lose out on the last part where the straights are. It meant that we outqualified Ferrari reasonably comfortably.

Pole in Canada is particularly important because the circuit, named after Jacques' father Gilles, is pretty mundane, and difficult to gain a big advantage on. It produces predictable grids, and this year it meant we had the front of the grid comprising pairs of cars: the two Williams, the Ferraris, the McLarens and the Benettons. I knew it would be very difficult to drive away from Jacques, that he would be there either in front or behind me if we were on the same strategy. I felt the start would dictate the pattern and, probably, the result of the race. If I stayed ahead, I had a good chance of being there at the finish.

Looking at the strategy, it seemed two stops would be much quicker than one, but Jacques decided he wanted to do just the one, and I was almost tempted to follow suit. If he'd gone for two, I think I might have gone for one, because I felt I needed to do something different to have a chance. The only drawback with a two-stop strategy was that if Jacques jumped ahead of me at the start I'd have trouble attempting to pass him. I thought very hard about it, but then decided to gamble and go the two-stop route. This explained why, at the start, I went off my line to make sure he couldn't pass me. He went to go one way, I went to block him, and then I took my line after that. I simply couldn't afford to let him through at that point, and I was entitled to do everything I did. I know that Jacques later made some comments to the effect that he didn't like what had happened, but I seem to remember that at the Australian Grand Prix, in Melbourne, he'd felt entitled to do all the blocking he wanted. Racing drivers are notorious for having short memories!

I did what I had to do. The Williams team did a brilliant job, again, and we were free to race each other – Jacques and I – without any concern for Michael, because he was put out of the running before the start. I was aware of that and it certainly made it easier to concentrate on my own targets. In a race like that, when two drivers are on different strategies, you're racing against the clock to make sure you have a gap that will enable you to come out ahead when you exit the pits after your final pit-stop. It worked out fine for me, and on the final stage I had the advantage of fresher tyres on the same sort of fuel load, and I was able to pull out a good cushion to win.

That victory gave me a lot of satisfaction. I'd won a good race, made all the right moves and recovered from the setback of two non-finishes. I left the circuit on a high as I rushed away to take a connecting flight from Montreal to New York to go home.

At the airport, after temporarily losing my passport and being refused permission to board the plane – carrying an expensive guitar I'd bought in New York – I'd arrived a little irritated in the departure lounge, where I was set upon by virtually every passenger. They all wanted my autograph. Fortunately, a good Samaritan airline lady whisked me off to her office, where I could reflect on a good result in peace.

They let me board the small-prop plane for the short hop to New York last, to give me a better chance to escape further attention. However, as soon as I boarded

That victory gave me a lot of satisfaction. I'd won a good race, made all the right moves and recovered from the setback of two non-finishes.

and went to take my seat the whole party broke into applause. From then on, I was signing autographs all the way to New York. Eventually the stewardess stood up and asked everyone 'to please leave Mr Hill alone, as he has had a hard day', but by then I must have signed all the requests for autographs it was possible to have.

Two days later I was testing at Silverstone, where I did sixty-eight laps on Wednesday and then sixty-three laps on Thursday. At the same time, Renault announced they intended to pull out at the end of 1997. I was partly prepared for this, as it had been talked about briefly beforehand. Naturally, it was a big talking-point once it was confirmed, raising the questions of how much effect it would have on this season and the next.

For 1996, all the real work had been done already, so I knew it wouldn't make that much difference. In 1997 it wasn't so much a question of whether Renault would start with a competitive engine, but of whether they would maintain it during the year. If it wasn't going well, they might think they were wasting their money. Apparently, Renault have a budget already for 1997, so it may be that they have a tremendous engine next year – we shall have to wait and see.

Naturally, at a pre-British Grand Prix media conference, I was asked how all this would affect my plans. I answered that it may have some bearing on them, which was a perfectly honest answer, but the next day it seemed everyone was reporting that I was ready to retire at the end of the year because of the engine situation. How you're supposed to get across any kind of answer without it being misrepresented is beyond me!

That Silverstone test gave us a chance to do a little more work on the latest Renault engine, which we'd used in Canada in practice, in readiness for the French Grand Prix. The developments this year have produced only very small improvements because Renault, like everyone else, have struggled with an airbox problem to improve their horsepower. The regulation changes, affecting the cockpit, mean that the air-flow to the roll-over bar, which doubles as the airbox, have been disturbed. This makes it difficult for the engine to breathe. When it's revving up to 16,000rpm, a three-litre Formula One engine is sucking in a hell of a lot of air – all of which it needs, so any disturbance becomes a real problem.

We went to France planning to race the new engines, a traditional move by Renault for their home race, for public relations reasons. But, honestly, if you'd blindfolded me and asked me to drive using both engines, I would have had a job to tell which was which. In truth, the new one was a little disappointing – there was no immediately discernible improvement.

I flew to a small airfield in France directly from Dublin with Georgie and Michael Breen. It was close to the track and made life easy. The atmosphere at the Magny-Cours circuit was also very relaxed and pleasant. It is set in rural France, in the middle of nowhere really, and is very spacious. Although it attracts a big crowd on Sunday, for the race, it does not create the pressure that goes with other venues and there is quite a casual atmosphere.

In all my years at the French Grand Prix, I'd always been on pole position but had never won. This time, I took the tongue-in-cheek line that maybe I shouldn't get pole; but, of course, that didn't stop me from trying. As it turned out, Michael Schumacher pulled it off, and left me to convince everyone that I was happy to try and win the race from second on the grid for a change. In all honesty, I was disappointed not to be on pole because I felt our car was far better than the Ferrari. We'd simply not got the best out of it.

Jacques, in his efforts to beat me in qualifying, had gone off, and was very lucky not to have been hurt. The television replay showed he'd kept his foot down when he was off on the grass, and he shunted quite heavily, rebounding on to the track where he narrowly missed hitting David Coulthard's McLaren Mercedes-Benz.

Obviously, Jacques didn't mean to do it, but he seemed quite impressed by his shunt. He had a kind of bravado, a bit of a gung-ho attitude which was a little bit unconvincing. I expected him to try and make light of the shunt, but he seemed impressed by it. He pulled about 10-G and said, 'That's not much, is it?' It's understandable to try and brush it off, but he was a lucky guy. Not only that, but he also strained his neck muscles quite badly.

Jacques bounces back from things like that, although his qualifying was affected. He had to start a couple of rows back, and he had his work cut out for the race if he wanted to try and beat me. For me, this was significant because the pattern of the championship was starting to develop, and I could see that he and Michael would be the main challengers. Michael had had a bad time in

> **The way things looked on the grid, it seemed that Michael rather than Jacques would be the main contender, but I couldn't have been more wrong.**

Canada, where Jacques finished second and scored points. The way things looked on the grid, it seemed that Michael rather than Jacques would be the main contender, but I couldn't have been more wrong.

Michael seemed to be brimming with confidence, almost overflowing with Germanic pride, in the pole position news conference on Saturday afternoon. A lot of comments were made about Germany winning Euro 96 – they played the Czech Republic the following day – and Michael had to answer questions about football. He talked about their injury problems, and said that if they needed him, he could play – which, I have to say, failed to raise a laugh. It was an attempted joke, but he capped it when someone asked him about his new clutch, a replacement for the one which had let him down in Canada, and he said he expected to get off the line this time because the new one had been made in Germany. It was all a bit too much for me, and by that point I wanted to go. It was a typical Michael performance.

The following day, I had an even more unpleasant experience to endure when I had a really bad warm-up session. It really couldn't have been any worse. I was fiddling around in my cockpit, making a few adjustments, when I made a novice's mistake on the back straight. I took my attention away from what was going on around me, and when I got to the hairpin and turned in I missed seeing Heinz-Harald Frentzen in his Sauber coming up on the inside. BUMP! I soon knew he was there.

I felt the impact, and there he was with three wheels on his waggon – and I had a damaged suspension. I returned to the pits, feeling embarrassed. I went out again, in the spare car, and as I went down the pit-lane there was this guy, in front of me, crossing the road and limping. He was bald, and coming from the Sauber pit. I had to slam on the brakes – he seemed completely oblivious to me. As I got closer, I thought I recognised him as Peter Sauber!

After that little incident I went off on the rest of my warm-up when, a little further round the circuit, I realised the brake pedal had moved. It had become detached, so when I went into the chicane I had no brakes and went straight into the gravel. I didn't even do a lap in the spare car, and I was certainly not in a good frame of mind for the race. It was the warm-up from hell.

I remembered an incident a few years earlier with Michele Alboreto, when he had driven me off the road in Hockenheim to get his own back for an incident at Magny-Cours (I'd gone inside him and he went off), so I decided to go and see Frentzen straightaway. I told him it was my fault and he was as nice as pie about it. Max Welti was there, too, so I asked him how Peter's leg was … He looked perplexed. Peter has two perfectly good legs, he told me.

In the drivers' pre-race briefing, I was standing next to David Coulthard, telling him how I had completely messed this up, when Roger Lane-Knott, the race director, came and said: 'What was Frentzen doing? The man's a maniac!' I'd just told David it was all my fault, so he rocked with laughter when he heard me tell Roger: 'Oh, yes. Frentzen? Definitely.'

Jacques was quickest in the warm-up, but he was down in sixth place on the grid. My big worry was Michael, but nothing prepared me for what happened. It must go down as one of the worst performances in Ferrari history. We were on the formation lap when Michael came out of the hairpin, having gone round only three corners, when

> **My big worry was Michael, but nothing prepared me for what happened. It must go down as one of the worst performances in Ferrari history.**

his engine blew up. Initially, I was trying to check how much oil was pouring from his car because I knew I'd be the first man into it on the next lap. Then I realised I was starting, effectively, from pole position again.

I got to the first corner first, made the most of it and, thereafter, it was pretty straightforward. I pulled away from Jean Alesi and won the race. It was something of a formality. Jacques put in some quick laps after going past Alesi, but I was able to maintain a ten-second lead over him, and we ended up with a Williams one-two. It gave me a 25-point lead in the championship, and Renault a one-two-three-four finish. On top of Michael's pre-race retirement, Ferrari lost Eddie Irvine after five laps. If they'd thought things were bad in Canada, their cup of misery had overflowed in France! At the end, when someone asked me what I thought when I saw Michael's car pulling off, I said I thought it might have been his German clutch.

Everything fell into place for me, and I had the perfect run-in for the British Grand Prix at the half-way stage in the season.

8 🏁 BRITAIN

After the French Grand Prix, everyone expected that my winning the championship would be a mere formality. It meant there was a new kind of pressure on me, something I had not experienced before. I arrived home late on Sunday night, had a day off to rest and recuperate, and then I went to test at Silverstone for three days: final preparations for the British Grand Prix.

When I got home after that, to really ensure I was going to be at my best for the British Grand Prix, I brought Erwin back to Ireland with me, and he flew his wife and their baby over too. I did four days of intensive training. We were in the gym for up to six hours a day – very serious work. Then, I had an afternoon off before flying, on the Tuesday before the British race, to Brands Hatch for a Rothmans promotional day. It was my first meeting with the mass media in the build-up to the

British Grand Prix, and I guessed they were not going to leave me alone for the next week. I was right.

Rothmans had hired Brands Hatch to get some filming done for themselves. Jacques and I drove a few laps for them and then we did a morning of interviews with media from all over Europe. I was asked repeatedly if I was going to win the British Grand Prix, to which I could only answer 'Yes, of course I am.' But I had to remind them all that a 25-point lead didn't mean I was certain to win the title. You can't count on anything, I explained, and while it may be a good lead, if Jacques was to win and I didn't finish, he'd be ten points closer. I didn't realise how prophetic I was being.

While all this talking was going on, they had opened up the circuit to the public, and a crowd of about 5,000 people had turned up to see the cars and their drivers! There were great cheers every time I came out of the garage, where the interviews were taking place. It was an entertaining sort of day, and at the end of it, Jacques and I did a simulated race start – so everyone went home happy. Then, finally, I was able to escape.

On Wednesday, I relaxed and played tennis and then went to open a race equipment shop in Chiswick owned by Ray Bellm. He had sponsored me when I raced bikes, and his family ran a pharmaceutical company. One of its products was Mucron catarrh tablets, a name which stuck in my memory because it was emblazoned on my leathers and my bike, and I became known to all who suffered from excessive mucus, but it did pay for my racing season. I did this opening as a thank-you for what he'd done for me back in 1983, and there was a good crowd there. It is an excellent shop, but, of course, it was also another media event, something I didn't want too many of as I needed to keep things under control in the build-up to the race.

The following day there was a news conference at Silverstone, where everything was well organised and as casual as possible. I was light-hearted and, knowing I would be scrutinised and interrogated by the media all weekend, took the view that I would enjoy myself and not allow myself to be hassled. As usual, there had been a lot of hype. The circuit was sold out for the race and expectations were high.

> **I was light-hearted and, knowing that I would be scrutinised and interrogated by the media all weekend, took the view that I would enjoy myself and not allow myself to be hassled.**

I had a good understanding of the way Nigel Mansell used to feel about the British Grand Prix. I had arrived as championship leader, I was expected to win and I had to perform like a winner in every respect.

For me, this was new territory. I led the championship in 1995, but only for one race and not at the time of the British Grand Prix. By the time of the French Grand Prix, this year, I felt things were being cemented into place. My win in France felt like a significant result, and I knew that a British victory would add some finishing touches; but I knew too that a non-finish would throw it open again, back to the kind of situation we were in after the first four races. It was all a different kind of pressure to be under for me, but I felt prepared and ready for it. To be honest, I enjoyed it. It was what I was there for – to win races and to win the championship.

Of course, there were all sorts of headlines about my future, some saying that I wanted £12 million to stay at Williams. I didn't read the papers so I had nothing to say about it – I hadn't thought about my future, my contract for next year or anything like that. I was happy with what I had, and was simply aiming to win a race and to go on and take the title. When people asked me what it would feel like to win the championship, what it would mean to me, or how much it would mean for 1997, I just told them that I really didn't know because I hadn't got that far yet! I could only think about the journey, not the destination. And I was determined not to allow anyone to get past me on the way.

I did think for a moment about going to see outside sources for a little extra advice – someone, for example, like Alain Prost. But I felt in the end that it would just end up confusing the issue. I had to deal with it in my own way. My motivation was extra-strong for Silverstone and the British Grand Prix. I was determined to do well and badly wanted pole, which I did in an exciting session on Saturday afternoon. It teed me up nicely for the race, and left Jacques looking pretty hacked off.

He wanted revenge for Canada, where I had upstaged him on his home turf. Revenge could be too strong a word for it, but I could sense his determination to beat me at Silverstone. There was no question about it. I had out-qualified him at every race of the season, and I think the fact that there had been a lot of speculation about his future position at Williams, in the weeks preceding the race, only added to his determination.

He knew also that I had no advantage over him at Silverstone because he knew the track and had been quicker than me in the tests leading up to the race weekend. On the other hand, I knew I tended to save myself for the events, rather than test laps, these days. That Saturday night was the first time all season I'd seen him so tired and down-in-the-dumps, but I knew he'd be back up for the race. One thing I have learned is that at this level of competition you can't discount people when they seem down. They just don't and won't give up.

It was against this background that I considered the race and our strategy. I knew Michael Schumacher was behind us, and that both he and Jacques were disappointed with their qualifying. In our pre-race discussions, we took Ferrari into account, but it was clear also that things were changing in other ways: the emphasis in our meetings was different because it was becoming clearer and clearer that the race, in terms of the championship, was going to be between me and Jacques. I knew Silverstone was a crucial race, and I knew I had to be well prepared and avoid becoming worn out before the start on Sunday afternoon. That is something that can happen

> **One thing I have learned is that at this level of competition you can't discount people when they seem down. They just don't and won't give up.**

easily at your home race, if you are not careful. I had to guard against being overworked.

For example, after each practice and qualifying session on Friday and Saturday, we had to go to the Paddock Club to see all the sponsors. Ours include Cellnet (my personal sponsors), Andersen Consulting, Rothmans, Renault and Elf, and I have to dash around and meet all the guests. On Sunday, however, it all happens before the event. I had time for a few interviews, when I was able to make a few jokes and relax and enjoy myself a little, and also to have a bit of fun with Murray Walker on the drivers' parade lap. Murray came in our car, perched on the back, and he paraded his OBE, waved to all the fans and I gave him a kiss and a bunch of flowers. The whole way round the circuit, he was revelling in it. 'This is *incredible*, abso-lute-ly *in-cred-ib-le...*' It was typical Murray.

After that, I had to take Tony Blair and his wife round the circuit. Cherie Blair loved it, but Tony kept apologising for doing this to me just before the race. He was actually a really charming guy, but he was hounded by the press as much as I was. Then I went back and did the public appearances for the sponsors before returning to the paddock to find that Bernie Ecclestone wanted me to take the Blair children round the track as well. This time I took the Renault out and threw it around, and the kids loved it. After I'd taken the entire Blair entourage around the track, it was time to come back and talk about racing.

All of this was after the warm-up and before the race, and shows the kind of hectic schedule we operate. The build-up was busy, and by this time I needed something to eat. Jacques had finalised his strategy and he knew exactly what he was going to do at the start. I knew my plans too – I wanted to lead the race and I wanted to win.

We ran through the final briefings and preparations and, very soon, were on the grid and the race was ready to start. When the lights went out my initial start – or the first part of it – was perfect, but then, unexpectedly, the rear tyres gripped much better than I thought they would. The revs dropped and, although it was nothing like the problem I had in Germany, it was a serious setback. I had to jump the clutch to stop the engine from stalling, but in doing so, I started to spin and went nowhere. In these kind of circumstances, you just don't get two goes at it – you get just the one, and if it doesn't work out, you're in trouble. I put all my efforts into it, but Jacques had gone and that was to be the last I saw of him.

My plan then was to take my mind off what Jacques was doing and to gain as many points as I could. By racing against the guys in front of me, I was forcing myself into the right frame of mind to try and improve my points total. I was then fifth, but I was determined to improve on that. The first part of my new plan was achieved when Michael pulled off after two laps, which put me up to fourth. But then I got stuck behind Mika Hakkinen's McLaren, and it would have been an enormous risk to try and get past him.

On lap twenty-three I felt something strange with the way the car was steering. Then I heard a clunk as I went round Club corner, and spent the rest of that lap checking the suspension to see if anything was wrong. I couldn't find out what it was, and the longer I went the stranger the handling became. Then I started to think that maybe I had a broken front anti-rollbar. This would account for the fact that every time I turned the wheel I had to turn it more and more to get the car round the corner. It was a similar problem to the one I had in Germany the previous year. I remember thinking, 'I'm damned if I'm coming in and they can't find anything wrong with it,' so I pressed on and began to think it must be something in my imagination when, suddenly, it became quite apparent it wasn't. The problem was very real.

I felt vibrations. I got on the radio and told them there was definitely something wrong with the car. I got to Copse corner on lap twenty-seven, hit the brakes and felt what seemed to be a wheel-bearing problem. I thought it had seized up. When I braked, it was like putting a hand-brake on. In fact, I only had brakes on three wheels, and it threw me off the track immediately. Fortunately, there is plenty of gravel there at Copse and I was all right. I left the car and expected a dejected reaction from the crowd. To my astonishment everyone was clapping and cheering, but there's nothing like the feeling of being put out of a race. Everything you have psyched up for is gone. It is very deflating, and it's hard to smile and wave in such circumstances. But the crowd reaction I was given was so warm, it went a long way to easing the pain I felt inside.

When I returned to the garage, the team were, understandably, focusing their attentions on Jacques. I was out of the race – and although on one hand I wanted the team to enjoy some success, on the other I didn't want to lose the championship in the process. I said thank you to everyone in the team and got the hell out of there. I didn't want to stay longer than I had to, and by 4.30pm I'd left.

There'd been so much expectation of me winning that I knew if I had won I would have been the luckiest man on the planet. I am not a pessimist. I am a realist. I knew that the odds of winning every time from pole position were slim. The whole weekend had been built around me winning the race, but I knew it was really only a 50–50 chance. No better than that. Of course, I had visions of winning, but this dream would have to wait another year.

As I left it all behind, I began reflecting. At that time, if you averaged out my points advantage over Jacques, for the first ten races, it was something like sixteen points. It had been as high as twenty-five and as low as four, after the first race. I knew the key thing, with a lead of fifteen points, was simply to try and continue to perform well, even though it was all so unpredictable. At Silverstone, I knew I'd driven better in qualifying than I had in France and that, on even terms, I would have beaten Jacques. It was a weird position to be in, and I knew that just about anything could happen. Anyone can hole a two-foot putt with no pressure, for fun, but when it is for millions of dollars, two feet becomes twenty-two feet. From now on, I had to stay focused, stay cool and not crack under the pressure.

9 🏁 GERMANY

After Silverstone, I went on holiday with my family for a month, to a villa I had rented in the south of France. It was a chance to relax a little, to soak up some good weather and absorb the heat in a planned programme of acclimatisation and preparation for the German Grand Prix, at Hockenheim, and the Hungarian, at the Hunga-roring in Budapest. Both races were usually run in very hot weather, and I knew it would be wise to plan for that and, of course, to work on my overall condition for the challenges which lay ahead.

The villa, near Cannes, was also a convenient location for our next test session, held at the Paul Ricard circuit at Le Castellet, near Marseilles. Relatively speaking, it was just down the road, so I was able to stay in close touch with the family and, at the same time, continue doing my job. The test had been planned with Hockenheim – the fastest circuit on the calendar and the lowest downforce track we go to – very much in mind. Like the German circuit, Paul Ricard has long straights which put the onus on power and speed and, of course, the brakes. Knowing I was only fifteen points ahead of Jacques at this half-way stage of the season made me anxious to win again.

I'd never won in Germany, as I've explained in Chapter Four, but I had a hunch that this might be my turn. When I arrived at the circuit, however, my first impression was that I was walking into another weekend of misfortunes, and that my confidence might be misplaced. I was met by a barrage of media inquisitors wanting to know my reaction to a headline that had been plastered all over the front cover of *Autosport* magazine. The story claimed that Heinz-Harald Frentzen had signed for Williams for 1997, and that my future with the team was in doubt. You can imagine how I felt. I had reached a stage in the season, and in my career, where I had every reason to believe I was an established leading driver, not one who was down for the chop! Quite naturally, the press wanted to get to the bottom of it and were asking me what I was going to do. At the time I really believed the story was just a lot of hot air.

Sensational stories often seem to crop up on Thursdays,

at the start of a Grand Prix weekend. I was used to that happening, and this, of course, was the German Grand Prix and Frentzen is German, providing a convenient if illogical hook for the media. I felt angry, but more at the frenzied reaction to the story than anything else. I believed that after Sunday all this would be forgotten, so I stuck to my policy of trying to ignore the hysteria and concentrating instead on the day-to-day business of getting on with the race.

It is difficult for anyone to imagine, or for me to explain, how it feels when you turn up at a Grand Prix circuit for an important race meeting, when you're fighting for the world championship and have already won six races, you're all fired-up, and then you're faced with shock news like this. It is very difficult to keep your cool and avoid reacting; I don't think I'd be human if I didn't admit

> **It is difficult for anyone to imagine, or for me to explain, how it feels when you turn up at a Grand Prix circuit for an important race meeting, when you're fighting for the world championship.**

to feeling furious at any idea that my position with the Rothmans Williams Renault team was insecure.

Rather infamously, however, the *Autosport* prediction proved to be correct, although confirmation of my being surplus to Frank Williams' requirements for 1997 was not to come for another four weeks. A lot was said and written at that time about whether Frentzen had already signed to drive for Williams. Certainly, if he *had* signed, I had absolutely no knowledge of it – and neither Frank Williams nor Patrick Head had given me any hint that that was the case. I did not believe it, so I dismissed it. It was academic.

All this, at the start of the weekend, led not only to such a massive crowd of reporters squeezing into the Williams motor-home that parts of its structure broke under the strain, but also to a huge level of interest in the race. I had received a very enthusiastic reception from the German fans, most of whom know me quite well now after my years of rivalry with Michael Schumacher, and this made driving in and out of the circuit something of an experience. I'd like to think they were all after my autograph, but the hire-car took a bit of a beating and several cans of beer were emptied over the roof. I can only presume this was a mark of my newly-acquired popularity with them!

Many Germans have come to see me as the main rival to their hero over the last few years, but this year I chose to believe that the warmth of their reception for me was as much for my own achievements in 1996 as it was for my competition with Michael in the past. Without doubt there was a less threatening atmosphere towards me than in previous years, and I felt that something had changed in their attitude. I know also that the Damon Hill merchandise sells well over there, which can only be good news!

Simply put, Michael and I were not rivals for the title any more, and this meant there was much less animosity between us. My relationship with Michael himself was a little different. I suppose without the heat of conflict between us we had both cooled off a little. Besides, I knew I had enough to worry about in just trying to maintain my advantage over Jacques, without thinking about Michael Schumacher's relationship with me. I would have to beat both of them in qualifying if I was to start the race from the front.

Michael, of course, was there to give his all for his country. He wanted to put his Ferrari on pole position and stir up the passions of the huge crowd at the circuit – and he very nearly did just that.

There were only three minutes to go before the end of

Running the gauntlet of the Hockenheim crowds.

'Team Willie' celebrates a close one-two in Hungary.

The run down to Eau Rouge at Spa: one of the most daunting experiences in Formula One.

Hiking with Erwin Göllner in Austria, before the Portuguese GP.
Winning is all about having the right altitude…

My boys: Bob, Paul, Matthew and 'Sir' Les look splendid in their London
Rowing Club caps. They kept my rowlocks well oiled at Suzuka.

The key at Monza is to take just the right amount of kerb – and miss the ty

The crowning moment: winner of both the race and the champio

...ael and Mika Hakkinen do the honours with the champagne.

the session – he was fastest, and I was in fourth place with only one run left. I went out of the garage so late that the session ended just as I crossed the line to start my lap. The crowd thought it was all over and went mad, assuming Michael was on pole. But the rules are such that if you start your lap before the end of the session, when the flag is waved, then that lap will count. I knew I couldn't afford to make any errors or it would all be over, so I just concentrated as hard as possible on driving cleanly. As I came into the stadium section, everyone was holding their breath. I drove that last part of the lap as if the car was on rails, and as I crossed the line, my on-board lap-timer confirmed I'd done it – I'd beaten Michael's time and won pole. Never have I felt so tremendously jubilant in a racing car: I was shouting 'Yes! Yes! Yes!' over and again in my helmet.

I was punching the air with pleasure when the team came on the radio and told me not to celebrate too soon, because Gerhard Berger was still out on a fast lap in his Benetton. Gerhard managed to improve on Michael's time too, but not mine, and that meant I was confirmed on pole and Michael, who'd been expecting to be there only a few minutes before, was bumped back to third. It all went very quiet – except in the Williams garage.

151

On Sunday it rained before the race, but that didn't really affect anything. I wanted to make an improved start after what had happened at Silverstone, but unfortunately I had another poor getaway. It was only marginally better than the one at the British Grand Prix. The problem at Silverstone had been that I'd had too much wheelspin, but at Hockenheim it was the opposite. I had hardly any this time, and the revs dropped so low I didn't have enough acceleration. There is a fine line between making a brilliant start and what everyone thinks is a very poor start, and this one exemplified that perfectly, making me more certain than ever that I needed to do a lot of work with my engineers to find what I want for an excellent start every time.

> **My plan was to stop twice, a strategy which was designed to give me the chance to attack in the closing stages, but unfortunately these intentions were undone when I was held up by a back-marker in the middle section.**

As a result of my less-than-ideal beginning to the race, I was left to run in third place behind the Benettons in the early stages, and there was a lot of communication back and forth between me and the team at the pit-wall. My plan was to stop twice, a strategy which was designed to give me the chance to attack in the closing stages, but unfortunately these intentions were undone when I was held up by a back-marker in the middle section. We reached a chicane together at a time when the yellow flags, which forbid overtaking, were out. As a result I think I lost about three seconds overall.

Later, after my pit-stop, I came out two seconds behind Gerhard and was left to curse that lost time as it became apparent to me that passing this very seasoned Austrian driver was not going to be an easy task. Gerhard knew exactly what he was doing, where and how to block me, and he understood the performances of our respective cars – which had the same Renault engines and straight-line performance – so well that he was able to retain his lead and stop me passing. I'd had dinner with him earlier that week, and I knew from our conversation then how determined he would be to secure what he regarded as an unlikely victory. I wasn't at all surprised, therefore, that he defended his position so resolutely. He is a very experienced driver.

On a high-speed track like Hockenheim, you have to be very careful not to get too close to the car in front at the wrong time. If you do get too close, you lose all the front end of the car because it becomes artificially light, and that makes it difficult to turn or stop because the front wheels have less grip. The car in front is sucking you into its tail. You can accelerate up to the car ahead, then be caught in its vacuum and find, quite suddenly, that you're accelerating much more quickly again. It's a very tricky situation, and very easy to get too close. If you lift off the accelerator you may slow down enough, but it's a difficult balance to keep – and at those speeds you really have to keep your wits about you.

It's not unknown for people to slipstream up to cars and, just as they are about to overtake, find they clip the back of the car in front. This happened to Christian Fittipaldi when he hit his Minardi team-mate's car at Monza in 1993 – and lifted off into an alarming aerial backflip through 360 degrees.

I knew all the dangers, but I still had to push as hard as I could on this very fast circuit, where we run at more than 200mph on the long straights and brake just 150 metres from the corner. When braking that late, you feel the car is going to stand on its nose each time, especially at the chicanes, where we pull something like 4-G under hard braking. With all these risks in mind, my main concern was ensuring that I finished the race, but I still wanted to put Gerhard under as much pressure as I could. He made the occasional mistake, but then recovered and drove in the middle of the track, waiting to see which side I tried to pass him on before moving across to shut me out.

There was no question he was driving to win, as he did all in his power to keep me behind him. I trusted him and never once expected him to do anything silly as we raced together at high speed, locked in a battle for victory. Then, coming out of a chicane, I heard a strange noise, a misfire, and because we were running so close I thought at first that it had come from my car. I was wrong, as I soon realised when I saw that Gerhard was going over to the left, leaving me to move to the right just before the guts of his car's engine poured out all over the track. I just managed to avoid being sprayed by the oil and spinning off, which was a distinct possibility in that situation. But once I got past that hazard, I was free to drive to the end without pressure and thoroughly enjoyed the sensation, although I was still a little concerned that my engine could go the same way as Gerhard's. I aimed my car at the Williams team as they hung over the pit-wall to cheer me across the line – a win, at last, in Germany.

I met my old friend Placido Domingo again at the podium ceremony, and also the tennis star Boris Becker. But it was the ten points I'd collected which really made my day. I thought back to Thursday, and all the hullaballoo about me losing my job, and I thought to myself, 'They can't possibly kick me out now. To win makes everything right again!'

Wrong!

> **I aimed my car at the Williams team as they hung over the pit-wall to cheer me across the line – a win, at last, in Germany.**

10 🏁 HUNGARY

I felt pretty good as I travelled back to the south of France after my win at Hockenheim. Not only had I rectified a notable omission on my CV, having won a Grand Prix on German soil for the first time, but I also felt I was back in control of the championship and, therefore, my own destiny. I felt things were looking good, that I had sent the doubters packing, and that I could enjoy a well-deserved ten days' holiday. But I was also telling myself not even to dream beyond the next race because, as I knew full well, Formula One has a nasty habit of turning round and biting you when you least expect it – as I was later to discover in no uncertain terms.

As it was, I decided to make the most of my chance to enjoy the sunshine, the beautiful surroundings and the opportunity to be with my family and some friends. Although in many ways we have an enviable lifestyle in

Formula One, we also have to spend a lot of time away from home and work very hard. Everyone involved in the sport has to put in long hours, and a lot of time is eaten up by travelling, waiting in airports and living in hotels. I was very keen, therefore, to make the most of my chance to enjoy a change of routine, although I could never allow thoughts of the team, the car or the next race – the Hungarian Grand Prix at the hot, dusty and twisting Hungaroring – to leave my mind.

All the time, while I was enjoying going out in boats, swimming in the pool, sitting in the sun or playing tennis, the Budapest race was never far from my thoughts. It was easy to understand why: not only did I have a lot to think about, for myself, but it was also the event at which the team hoped to clinch the constructors' championship for a record-equalling eighth time. On top of that, it was the race at which I was to be shadowed, just about every-where – whether I liked it or not – by the journalist and TV presenter Clive James and his camera crew.

Clive was making a film, to be shown in 1997, based on three weeks of my life from the Hungarian race through to the Belgian race at Spa, a time when the championship was boiling towards a serious scrap and the traditional Formula One silly season was getting into full swing. I was pretty much surrounded by microphones and cameras for two whole weeks, but I did my best to stay calm all the time, whatever was going on around me.

Clive is an intelligent, amusing and well-read man. However, he was there to work on his documentary, and I wanted to make sure I made the most of my family days, so it was rare for us to find the time to enjoy each other's company. I had no testing planned before flying to Hungary so I did everything I possibly could with the children (I am actually not much good at sitting down and doing nothing anyway!). We took the opportunity to enjoy the Mediterranean – I borrowed a Sunseeker powerboat for a couple of days – and I spent a lot of time in the swimming pool trying, successfully I am proud to say, to teach the children to swim. I have strong feelings about this, as I learned to swim from an early age and I love being in the water: snorkelling, swimming, water-skiing and so on. But more importantly, the boys now have a chance to save themselves if it ever came to that. People talk about the stress of my job, but, believe me, it's nothing compared to looking after a swimming pool full of under-fives.

The hot weather also helped me acclimatise to the heat we expected to face in Hungary, so I felt in very good shape when I arrived in Budapest for the race and for my weekend under the all-seeing eyes of Clive James' cameras. They were everywhere. I had a microphone stuffed up my shirt most of the time, as well as a camera in my face … They filmed me eating breakfast, staring at the wall, scratching my head, going to the toilet – or at least it seemed as if they did! – and doing just about everything in between. Clive kept popping up in all sorts of places to ask typically awkward questions, which often prompted some entertaining banter. I don't know what will be kept in and edited out, but it should make for quite a revealing film.

Clive's presence, however, was only one of the distractions which take up time at a Grand Prix. Although it was enjoyable I was well aware of the job ahead: I had focused my mind during our holiday, and I knew what sort of challenge to expect and how to go about the task. While Williams wanted to win the constructors' title, which of course I was keen to contribute to fully, I must admit I was more concerned with my challenge to win the drivers' title.

It is always Williams' goal to win the constructors' prize. Frank Williams and Patrick Head regard it as their target each year, and they take the view that the drivers' championship is there for the drivers to win. Given that I was in my sixth year with the team, and felt very much a part of it, I had a strong feeling that I had contributed to their success – and I wanted to carry on doing so. I'd been a Williams driver from the start of my career in Formula One and I felt a kinship with the team. Of course, I wanted to win the race for myself, but I wanted to win it for Williams as well.

It was almost certain that we'd win the constructors' championship, and since Sunday night is impossible for celebrating, because everyone hits the road, I invited the whole team out for a big dinner on the Thursday night, at a very good Italian restaurant. We had a huge table and I ended up with a very large bill, but I'd wanted to do it and hadn't been able to invite everyone out like that since Brazil. Drivers are often accused of having short arms and long pockets, but these days there are so many people working in a Grand Prix team it is almost impossible to do this kind of thing at all. There are about 220 people in total at Williams Grand Prix Engineering, so you'd need a hell of a table to invite them all. I asked everyone I could, including all the guys from Renault Sport. I even asked Jacques!

The Hungaroring is always a busy place, usually hot, and one of the most physically demanding places we go to. But I like it – I nearly always perform well there: I won my first Grand Prix there, in 1993, and I won again in 1995. The Williams team also had a very good record in Hungary, so I felt confident about our prospects and preparations. Jacques had done testing for the race the previous week at Nogaro, and I knew he'd be up for it. We wanted to do well, to take the constructors' title and do it in style. The Williams cars went perfectly, as usual, but there was proof of the progress our rivals were making in seeing Michael Schumacher put his Ferrari on pole position. I'd sensed that the competition was getting closer and closer, and this proved it. It was a disappointment, but the fact that Jacques was third meant something else as a result – I had the worst side of the worst grid of the year for the start.

Of all the places we go to, the Hungaroring has the most notoriously slippery grid. Off the racing line, which is cleaned by constant use during practice and qualifying, it is filthy dirty and covered in dust. This makes it very difficult to get away cleanly.

I knew that even if I made a peach of a start – which, given my most recent efforts, looked doubtful – I was still going to have difficulty going through the first corner in front of Michael. And, if that happened, I knew it would cause problems, because if you can't get a clear track in Hungary, you have to just sit and watch and wait … and hope the guy in front makes a mistake. If he doesn't, you have to wait for the pit-stops or suffer the frustration of hoping for something to go wrong for him all the way to the flag.

On race morning I tried my best to clean up the line by going over and picking up the dust, but it didn't make much difference. I thought it was worth attempting something, but I knew that the real problem on that circuit was that the left-hand side of the track is the place to be – and the right-hand side is the place not to be. When the lights went out, I made a reasonable 'initial' start, but as soon as the tyres started to roll I had a lot of wheelspin. I could do nothing about it and slipped backwards from second to fourth. Jean Alesi, whose getaways had been improving all through the summer, made a fantastic start in his Benetton and jumped ahead of me.

Jacques, starting from the left where the grip was much better, took second place. So, on the first lap, it was Michael, Jacques, Jean and myself. Unfortunately, Alesi was a lot slower than both Jacques and Michael, and I was stuck behind him for the whole of the first section of the race. On a track like the Hungaroring, where the grip is so poor and the tyres take a real hammering, I knew it was vital to be able to meet the targets demanded by the strategy for the race. We'd decided on a 'four-sets' strategy, that is with three pit-stops, because tyre-wear is so high – but I also had the opportunity to be flexible and 'go through' if I wanted.

This meant that if the set-up on the car felt good enough I could have done the race with just two stops, by loading up enough fuel at the start to make the tactic possible. If, for example, I'd got ahead of Michael and then held him off, I think this strategy would have guaranteed me the race. But it didn't work out like that – and, to put it mildly, we had a little bit of confusion over our tactics during the race.

When Alesi came in for his stop, I stayed out, according to plan. I should have been able to go quicker than him then, even on my old tyres, because I had less fuel. So I stayed out and did a few more laps to try and make

> **Unfortunately, just as I was preparing to leave the pits after my refuelling and tyres stop, Eddie Irvine came in in his Ferrari. It meant I had to slam on the brakes to avoid hitting him, and that cost me one or two seconds – vital seconds …**

sure that when I did come into the pits I'd be far enough ahead to come out in front of him. I knew that was essential to give me a chance to push on with my own race and keep alive my hopes of victory. Unfortunately, just as I was preparing to leave the pits after my refuelling and tyres stop, Eddie Irvine came in in his Ferrari. It meant I had to slam on the brakes to avoid hitting him, and that cost me at least one or two seconds – vital seconds – because when I came out, and rejoined the race, there was a 'whoosh' and the one person I didn't want to see, Alesi, went by, just ahead of me, and right on my line. I was stuck behind him again! I could hardly believe it. Every lap I was stuck behind him I was losing around two seconds, and Jacques, who'd got ahead of Michael after the pit-stops, was pulling away at the front.

It was, to say the least, highly frustrating. I could see myself losing a lot of points to Jacques and I was just wondering how I was going to resolve the Alesi problem when it resolved itself – thanks to the dirty line which had caused me all the trouble at the start. Luckily for me, as we went past a back-marker on the start–finish straight, Jean had to go to the right, to the dusty side of the track, to get by. He picked up a lot of rubbish on his tyres, and as he went into the first corner he almost lost control. I was able to take advantage and slip through.

This meant I was up to third and could at last push on in the hope that I'd still play a major part in the outcome of the race. I really felt that another victory, which would have been my eighth of the season and an important blow in the drivers' championship, was still on for me. Before I pitted I'd asked over the radio if I should go to three stops, and Tim Preston had said, 'No, stick to the original plan' – which I took to mean a two-stop race. So, after my first pit-stop, and after passing Alesi, I really got the hammer down and flew round the track. I thought I had one less stop to make than Jacques, and I knew I was twenty-five seconds behind him. I really thought I had a chance.

I pushed and pushed and pushed. In the process, I made up a lot of time before, surprisingly for me, I became aware that the team wanted me to pit again, at around mid-distance. I hadn't expected this, so I was more than a little perplexed. I asked them how many stops I was doing, and they told me I was doing three. It was the first I'd heard of it since my talk with Tim, and I hit the roof! I couldn't understand it. I wanted to know why, because I thought they'd put enough fuel in for me to do a two-stop race, and I knew I could have caught Jacques. The race was still on, but I was being told to come in! I was bloody furious at the time and the language was pretty fruity over the radio. Stopping three times meant it would be impossible for me to win, but there was nothing I could do about Jacques taking points away from me. My main task, afterwards, was to get ahead of Michael and to take the six points for second place. Michael had a throttle problem, and wasn't going as quickly in the race as he had in qualifying. I tracked him down, closed in on him and, when he made a pit-stop, I got ahead. Then I really went for it again and set several fastest laps to close to within a second of Jacques when we crossed the line. It was a good result for the team, but a big disappointment for me.

I'd really driven as hard as possible to score those six points, but I knew I couldn't afford to be doing that any more. I had out-qualified Jacques, once again, but finished behind him because of a poor start. I was the fastest guy in the race, but it's no good being fastest if you finish second! I was less than happy, therefore, but the team had won the constructors' championship in style with a one-two and there was a lot of celebrating. The points gap between myself and Jacques was down from twenty-one to seventeen, and I was feeling pretty disillusioned. It could, and should, have been quite different.

I didn't have time after the race to go into the changes in strategy and the confusion over them in detail, because

I had to leave that evening for Bulgaria, where I was scheduled to make a promotional appearance for Rothmans. But I learned later that, despite what I'd felt (and said) during the race, they were quite right in putting me on to a three-stops strategy. They wanted to find a way of getting me ahead of Alesi, and it would have worked fine if it hadn't been for me being held up by Irvine. That's where the plan went wrong. Of course, it is easy to analyse these things after the event and I have to admit that, by and large, the strategy was correct because, above all else, the team were still racing to win the constructors' championship and they wanted to see me move ahead of the Benetton. The only thing I was annoyed about in the end was that I hadn't been told over the radio that I was on a three-stop strategy, when I thought I was on two.

It was an important win for Jacques, psychologically, and he was duly feted for it. But I honestly felt I had him under control, and that it should have been me on top of the podium. If I could have put pressure on him, I think I would have beaten him. Jacques drove a great race to hang on to his lead, but I was only within reasonable striking distance over the last six laps or so and never really had a chance to push him to his limits. But when we got out of the cars after the race he said, 'Jeez! You were really going fast at the end!' As fast as I damn well could, I thought.

The result meant that the championship was becoming more of a cliff-hanger for us both, but I remained very confident that I'd win it. I had a strong feeling that when the chips were down, I was the one with much more in reserve. I knew, too, that we were in for a big race again at Spa, where Jacques had never raced and I had the advantage of experience. So, although I was disappointed, my confidence was still intact as I hurried away from Budapest towards Bulgaria for the Rothmans hit-and-run personal appearance. I knew there was still a long way to go before the end of that day – and before the end of the championship, too.

> **Jacques said, 'Jeez! You were really going fast at the end!' As fast as I damn well could, I thought ...**

11 🏁 BELGIUM

The journey to Bulgaria, and my first evening there, were memorable experiences. I'd driven as hard as I could in a Grand Prix for an hour and forty-five minutes and then had to dash, nearly as fast, to get to the airport in time for the flight. It was important to make the connection that night, immediately after the race, because I had the Rothmans promotional appearance to do as soon as I arrived. Such is the high-living jet-set lifestyle of a Formula One racing driver!

To make sure I didn't miss the flight I was given a motorcycle escort around the back-streets of Budapest, with sirens blaring, so any poor unfortunates who happened to be there were forced to leap out of the way. The idea, of course, was to avoid all the traffic pouring out of and away from the Hungaroring. The Hungarian Grand Prix had attracted one of its biggest ever crowds – mostly

Germans who had gone there in the hope of seeing Michael Schumacher win. But we managed to find a way through them all and made it to the airport in about forty minutes which, I thought, was bloody good going. And we were still in one piece at the end of it all – a small miracle in itself!

Then we climbed aboard our jet and took off for Varna, together with Clive James and his crew in tow. Varna is a resort on the Black Sea, the Bulgarian equivalent, I suppose, to Cannes. When we arrived, it was immediately obvious that there was plenty of night-life there, as we were whisked off to the Rothmans night-spot where I was scheduled to hand out prizes to those who had won a competition on a Rothmans driving simulator. There was a lot of loud music and shouting: a typical seaside resort atmosphere. The whole crowd seemed to be having a great time and they gave me a truly fantastic reception. I think everyone was as surprised as I was that I was actually there – only six hours after climbing out of my racing car.

It was enjoyable, but tiring, on top of the weekend I'd just been through. The strain at a Grand Prix is as much mental as physical, as the concentration levels are so high, so sponsor functions like this directly after a race are not quite what I'd normally do, given the choice. But, having said that, I appreciated the opportunity I had to visit Bulgaria.

The following day there was a full-scale press conference and then a series of radio and television interviews. By the time it was over, I was glad to have the prospect of flying back to the south of France to look forward to. It was all rather exhausting and, meanwhile, I had the Clive James crew there just to catch me in those moments when it seemed I had nothing to do.

I had two days before testing started in Barcelona, so I fitted in the experience of a lifetime by visiting Marineland and swimming with some dolphins – not something I do regularly, despite my love of water-sports. But when I was offered the chance I just had to go for it. The dolphins were in the charge of John Kershaw, who guided me through the do's and don'ts. The first don't was: 'Don't jump when they bite your toes – it only encourages them to do it again.' Fair enough, I thought, just as long as I still have my throttle foot left when I've finished my swim! Only when you take a close look at their teeth do you realise just how benign and tolerant these animals are towards humans. They make us look pretty shameful as a species when you see how gentle they can be, especially with children. Mind you, they'll do anything for something to eat!

On Thursday I went testing at the Circuit de Catalunya, doing eighty-seven laps that day followed by a further fifty on Friday, during which I did some work on my starts. Then I flew back to France for one more day's rest before going home to Ireland and another Rothmans appearance, in Phoenix Park, Dublin, in front of about 80,000 people. I gave some prize-winners a ride around the track in a Renault Spider, then did some more interviews with Clive James on Monday (yes, he was still around!). I then had a couple of days at home before travelling to Spa.

By the time I got to the circuit, in the beautiful Belgian Ardennes forest, my and Jacques' starting techniques (Jacques used a hand-clutch and left-foot braking) were the talk of the paddock. Everyone was asking about our starting styles and, quite obviously, they'd all become overnight experts! It was a classic example of how journalists can latch on to something, whatever it is, and dig their teeth into it and refuse to let go. I didn't think it was worth all the fuss that was made, but there was nothing I could do about it.

The fight between me and Jacques for the drivers' championship was the real focus of the weekend. Jacques had never been to Spa before, but he arrived in a confident frame of mind knowing he had closed the gap. On the other hand, I knew that I could afford to finish second to him in every race and still win the championship, by one point. Naturally I didn't *want* to win it that way – my approach was that if I won at Spa and Monza then it was all over, so I went into the weekend with the view that I was there to win the race and nothing else. Jacques was pretty focused too, and inevitably a lot of people began to ask questions about our working relationship and the rising tension between us – something that everyone just seemed to assume existed.

The truth is that the relationship between Jacques and me was the same all through the season. He did his thing and I did mine, but that was not a major problem for me and there were never any real differences, or difficulties, between us.

I did find, however, that it was quite a strange experience to have a championship battle with someone from inside your own team rather than with someone from another team. It meant we were concentrating on different things rather than a mutual target. I felt it screwed us a little in Spa, because we spent too much time looking at each other rather than the others. In other circumstances I think we'd all have performed much better.

It was an odd weekend because of that. We were both working to find the best possible set-ups and I felt I had found one that made me feel as confident as I'd ever been for a race at Spa. I was really enjoying the car and the speed of the corners, particularly Blanchimont, which we were taking at more than 300kph – nearly 190mph!

Spa, of course, is notorious for its changeable weather. We had a weather-man with the team, and he told us that it would rain within the first ten minutes of qualifying, so everyone queued up in the pit-lane for the start to try and put in an early 'banker' lap in case the clouds opened. It meant that when you got on to the track you had to try and separate yourself from the crowd a little, to find a bit of clear track to lap quickly for a usable time. I was able to go faster than Jacques, but it was Gerhard Berger who was fastest, at that early stage, in his Benetton.

This was interesting. Jacques had been quick over the two previous days and had impressed many people because it was his first visit to the circuit. But I was not unduly worried. He'd heard a lot about Spa and I knew he was looking forward to it. He likes to go quickly – any driver who can lap Indianapolis at 240mph or something like it must be a speed freak – and he thought the track would suit him. It did, and he was quick straight-away for a change: usually he trundled around on the first day, finding his rhythm, but this time he went out with the obvious intention of doing his best, because he had nothing to lose and needed to win. He attacked the circuit. But I was happy for him to have his head because I wanted to keep something up my sleeve for qualifying, some reserve, and I knew that it is always more demoralising to lose out in the last moments. I out-qualified him on the first run, but he out-qualified me on the second, taking provisional pole. I looked at the sky and realised it was time to go again, quickly, because it was about to rain. Jacques also went and did a quick time on that run, four-tenths faster than mine, and timed it well; my third run was too late, spoiled by the rain. I wasn't able to get the lap right and cursed myself as I realised that, because of the rain, it was unlikely I'd get another run in the dry – and therefore Jacques would have out-qualified me for the first time since Melbourne.

It was not as I'd hoped it would be, but I tried not to be too disappointed. I was still on the front row, and we

> **I was really enjoying the car and the speed of the corners, particularly Blanchimont, which we were taking at more than 300kph – nearly 190mph!**

were well clear of Michael's Ferrari, with everyone else even further back. As Jacques was ahead of me, he was able to have first call on the pit-stops. This meant there was a bit of a deadlock on Saturday night, as neither of us wanted to discuss how many stops we wanted to do. Each wanted to see what the other did first.

In the event, we both decided to do two stops. We also felt we were struggling, very slightly, for straight-line speed, so we decided to reduce downforce. I took off the same amount as Jacques because I knew I couldn't afford to be slower than him. It was a critical decision. I talked it over with Adrian Newey and the Renault guys, and we discussed what we thought would be the optimum wing level. It is always difficult to make exactly the right decision, but I couldn't afford to give Jacques any kind of advantage and I believed that if he stopped first, and I went on for two more laps, I would get ahead. So I planned my race like that – to stop two laps after Jacques, but to carry more fuel on the car at the start. I knew, of course, that I had to stay with him in the first section to make this strategy pay.

Things went well in the warm-up, but then … it rained. In fact, it rained so heavily that they decided to organise a special session to acclimatise to the wet. Then, typical of Spa, it dried out quickly and the session was called off, which meant that we went to the grid on a damp surface with sunshine around most of the rest of the track. Unfortunately, the way the circuit drains at Spa, my side of the grid was wet – and Jacques' was dry. I knew I needed a good start, but how could I if I was on slick tyres on a wet part of the track? I was praying for the sun to beat down and dry it all up!

We went off on the formation lap, and when we rolled back on to the grid there was still a wet patch about two car-lengths in front of me. When the lights went out I got off the line well, but as soon as I hit the wet patch I lost traction – and that was enough for Michael to slip through as we ran up towards the hairpin. As we got there, Jacques braked a little too late and slid wide. He started to take Michael with him and I thought I could slip down the inside and get through, but they managed to hold their advantage. So, as we headed down the hill towards Eau Rouge, it was Jacques, Michael and me, and I knew that I just had to keep my foot down flat as I went barrelling down and into that corner. But I was so close to Michael that I just couldn't do it without losing downforce, and I dropped back out of it. This gave David Coulthard, in his McLaren Mercedes-Benz, a chance to go past me on the way up the hill. I'd dropped two places on the opening lap. It was later noted by

Renault engineers that my car had marginally lost power on the first lap, which may explain why David was able to go by so easily.

David actually began pulling away from me. I couldn't stay with him, and in my mirrors I could see Mika Hakkinen in the other McLaren, doing the same speed as me. I felt there was something wrong with my car: it was under-steering and I wasn't able to go as quickly as I wanted. On the other hand, I didn't want to do anything desperate, so I pressed on, just hoping that it might rain again – anything at all to shuffle the running order a little and upset the race. My prayers were answered – but not in the way I'd hoped – when something did happen: Jos Verstappen had a shunt at Stavelot.

He must have gone off just as Coulthard went through, because David didn't lose any time, but when I came round the corner there were yellow flags waving and tyres bouncing all over the track. I had to make a

> **I clenched my buttocks, because the floors of the cars are not noted for their strength and can be pierced easily, and held on tight!**

sudden decision on which way to go, and managed to squeeze between two tyres rolling across the track in front of me. That meant I had to run over a piece of suspension lying on the circuit, a decision I'd taken instinctively when forced to choose between hitting either a tyre or, possibly, the debris. I clenched my buttocks, because the floors of the cars are not noted for their strength and can be pierced easily, and held on tight! I remember, about four years ago, in testing at Estoril, that J. J. Lehto had driven over someone's abandoned drive-shaft, and it had penetrated his car and come up between his legs. He was a bit white-faced after that experience ... But, mercifully for me, my car went straight over the piece of suspension without damage.

I did one more lap like that before the safety car came out, and then I decided it was time to come in. The team came on the radio and said, 'Pit, Damon, pit,' but just after committing myself to enter the pit-lane they came back on and said 'Stay out, stay out!' I had no choice but to go left, which meant I had to weave through the polystyrene barriers that prevent cars rejoining the track at high speed, and then be held up by a marshal holding a board until the track was clear. During this wait both Mika and Gerhard went through ahead of me. I'd lost two more places. I could hardly believe it, but suppressed my anger as best I could. I knew it would be useless to lose my temper now, and I wanted to keep my wits about me – but I was very miffed, to put it mildly.

I made my pit-stop on the next lap, but by then everyone else had been in and I ended up down at the back of the queue. As far as I could see, I was bog last and Jacques was first, and I wasn't even sure what had happened or why. Then Adrian came on the radio and said, 'Sorry, Damon, you're just going to have go for it now.' 'Thanks a lot, guys,' I replied, with, I felt, quite justifiable facetiousness.

I waited for the safety car to pull in. When it did, I was so far back I didn't actually see it happen, but I soon began to make up for it. I got past a few people on the first lap, but then I was held up behind Martin Brundle's Jordan Peugeot. It was difficult to get by him, and I knew that with every lap that went past the queue ahead was getting longer and more strung-out. Eventually, I got past Brundle and clawed my way back to sixth, which became fifth when Coulthard lost it. I had no idea then how important that extra point might be. Jacques had lost out in the pit-stops too, and could only manage to come second, but the result was the equivalent of him winning and me finishing second – the difference of four points was just the same. But psychologically there is a huge difference between how you feel after winning and how you feel after coming second. It wasn't the race either of us had expected and, in retrospect, I think we were both too wrapped up in watching each other – with the net result that neither of us did the right thing with our race set-ups. Consequently we looked pretty weak in the race. Even Gerhard Berger was faster!

Afterwards I had the rare experience of conducting my post-race interviews from the pit-lane rather than the media centre, where the top three finishers gather. I tried my best to be upbeat after what could only be described as a complete cock-up, considering our grid positions. Adrian, later, bravely and with rare honesty and selfless-ness, admitted that it was his fault that I'd ended up at the back of the safety-car queue. He was being too hard on himself. The reason I couldn't come in when I was first told to was that it had been pointed out to Adrian at the last minute that the pit-stop was set up for Jacques. The reason for this was that he'd misunderstood the radio signal to come in for his stop.

In hindsight, it would have cost me less time if I'd come in when originally told to, despite the fact that the team would have had to re-set the pit-stop equipment and tyres. All season I'd been trying to emphasise that we work as a team and we all take responsibility for our performance, but Adrian had to be congratulated for stepping forward like that. Apportioning blame was not on my mind. Jacques had taken four points away from me – and that was what was on my mind more than anything.

> **"** **'Thanks a lot, guys,' I replied, with, I felt, quite justifiable facetiousness. "**

12 ⚑ ITALY

It happened on Wednesday, August 28, while I was at home in Ireland. The phone rang. It was Frank Williams. Quite simply, he said: 'Damon, we won't be asking you to drive for us next year. It is not about money. I can't tell you much more, but I have to think about the future of the company as we'll be losing our Renault engines at the end of 1997, and I must consider how I'm going to get replacements – and I am not going to change my mind.' Michael Breen, my solicitor, had called a few minutes earlier to tell me that Frank had broken off negotiations and was going to call me himself. Michael had also told me then that Frank was not going to ask me to drive for him next year, so I was partly prepared for it, but it was still a shock. I felt the bottom had dropped out of my world. All the euphoria of being in the lead in the championship, the thrill of the race wins, suddenly seemed for nothing.

Michael and I had felt something was wrong after his first discussions with Frank. Our suspicions had then been raised by Frank's apparent lack of concern at one or two details we were asking for during the negotiations, and things had, generally, seemed a little unusual. It had seemed strange, too, that he hadn't wanted to start negotiating until such a late date in the year. It was August, after all, before we really began. Also, when Michael had asked about a few fundamental points, Frank had merely said, 'Oh, I'll have to ask Patrick about that …'

Once I'd put the phone down, my first feelings were of immense disappointment and sadness that I wouldn't be driving for the team I'd been with for six seasons. I felt I was just coming into my own as a driver in the Williams team. I felt I could have contributed as much to the team effort as any driver. Quite apart from anything else, I was leading the world championship, and had a very good chance of winning it and then defending the title in the number-one car. All this, however, was lost, because of Frank's decision.

By the Monday after Spa, Michael and I had come to the conclusion that Frank was possibly stringing us along, so we were on the point of giving him a deadline by which time he had to conclude our deal. But we never reached that point. Michael was supposed to have received a call from Frank on Tuesday, but when Frank called he simply delayed his response for a further day. He was supposed to phone to set up a meeting to discuss terms. Up until that time, we'd had a brief discussion in Budapest and Michael and Frank had had another meeting at the factory in Grove. Frank seemed very amiable and, in fact, had called me on the Monday before that meeting to say that Michael was coming up and that he was looking forward to it. He sounded very enthusiastic, and the meeting appeared to go well, although it was made clear at that time that anything was negotiable. They then had another meeting at Spa-Francorchamps. Frank explained that he was going to meet Michael again, and we were left waiting for him to call to finalise that discussion. When he eventually called on the Wednesday, it was only to end it all.

During the short call, I asked him when he had made the decision. He said 'an hour ago', but I had strong doubts about the truth of that. There had been plenty of smoke well before this fire, and it went back all the way to the Suzuka and Aida races in October 1995. There'd been rumours flying around the paddock even then that my drive had been taken by Heinz-Harald Frentzen. I knew I had a contract for

1996, but I was still worried. I had a feeling, right back then, the previous October, that something might be wrong, and I couldn't understand why all these stories, the rumours flying around, weren't being denied by Frank or Patrick. I was upset that they didn't say anything to defend me or my position with the team, especially at such a tough time and in view of the fact that I was supposed to be their driver for the following year.

On the Monday morning after the Aida race, the Pacific Grand Prix, I went to see Patrick Head and I asked him if they had signed Frentzen. He said no. I had an uncomfortable feeling about his response, but didn't dwell on it – I had other things to worry about at the time, like dealing with losing the championship. But when the rumours resurfaced strongly at the time of the German Grand Prix in July 1996, following a story in *Autosport* magazine, apparently from an extremely reliable source, it sounded all too familiar. Together with some other information that I had about the plans of a leading person at Williams, I began to believe that there might be something behind the Frentzen story, although at the time of the race, as described in Chapter Nine, I dismissed it.

There is no way I can be sure of the exact truth of how

or when Frank made his decision. One possibility is that he was upset by rumours in the press about the time of the British Grand Prix that I had spoken to Ron Dennis who, it was alleged, had offered me £10 million to drive for him. This would have been very nice, of course, but in fact I had stuck to my strategy of not entering into any negotiations for 1997 at all until the business of the 1996 season was settled. So those rumours were wildly inaccurate. At the start of the season, I set myself the goal of winning the championship, and I took the view that if I didn't win it then I'd be better off driving somewhere else next season.

I was, therefore, pursuing the principle – emphatically pressed on us by Frank in February – that he'd already lost two or three world champions and he wasn't

> **At the start of the season, I set myself the goal of winning the championship, and I took the view that if I didn't win it then I'd be better off driving somewhere else next season.**

going to make the same mistake again. He didn't like all the criticism he'd had to take from the sponsors and from Renault. Michael Breen and I both took him to mean what he said. We accepted his word. For the previous three years he'd held the upper hand – but, after all, he had given me my big break. I'd had the opportunity to win races, but I'd not been well paid (in Formula One terms) at that time.

Frank had always said that when my 'apprenticeship' was over, then I'd have my shot at getting paid properly. That's what he said – and, true to his word, in 1996 I *was* reimbursed properly. From my side, why should I have wanted to drive for any other team in 1997 when Williams would, most likely, have the most competitive car? It was simple: I wanted to drive for Williams. I'd said all year that I wanted to stay with them. Of course it would have done me no harm to have had an attractive alternative offer from, say, McLaren – but, in this instance, the speculation was no more than that.

Before the British Grand Prix, when Renault announced they were going to withdraw from Formula One, someone asked me how it would affect my plans for 1997. I replied that it may affect my thinking, but I didn't really know. I thought it was a straightforward and honest answer. I didn't know the details of the Renault announcement at the time and had no idea what their plans for 1997 were. My reply, seen by some as a hint that I was thinking of moving, sparked off the rumours that I might retire or that I might go to McLaren. I think, looking back, that it is possible these things may have had an effect on Frank and Patrick's thinking, if the deal with Frentzen hadn't already been done. They may deny it, but they have sensitive egos and may not have liked it to look as if they were being placed second to another team, or even to their driver.

During Silverstone weekend, I made it very clear to Frank that I had nothing to do with the rumours and nothing to do with what the newspapers were reporting. I told him, quite clearly, that I wanted to drive for Williams next year and that I wasn't talking to, or interested in, anyone or anything else. He said, 'Damon, I

> **During Silverstone weekend, I made it very clear to Frank that I had nothing to do with the rumours and nothing to do with what the newspapers were reporting.**

don't read the papers. They just go straight in the bin.'
But I know from my own experience that you don't
actually have to read the papers to know what is in
them. There are plenty of people willing to tell you
themselves!

It was also rumoured at that time that Frank was
trying to get out of his contract with Jacques. I heard
there was talk in that direction. A theory could be put
together that fits this story – which is that Frank *did*
sign Frentzen, as suspected, at the end of 1995, and that
mid-way through 1996 he was looking to get himself
out of the embarrassing situation of having to replace me
at the end of the year. But all this is just guesswork.
Whatever the truth is, I suspect that our negotiations
with Frank were a sham, and that he never had any
intention of carrying them through properly. Two brief
meetings simply did not constitute a proper negotiation
between us.

At the end of the day, however, I have to acknowledge
that it is Frank's team, that he is the boss and that he
makes the decisions. There was nothing I could do about
it. It was over. That was that.

Naturally, it was important for me to ascertain when
Frank wanted to make an announcement. He told me it
would be done on the Tuesday after Monza, but by

Friday afternoon, the week before Monza, the phones were ringing constantly and it was decided that this could not be kept quiet any longer. Michael called a news conference for Sunday to announce what was happening, and also to avoid a situation in which I would have turned up at Monza, fighting to win the championship, with an axe over my head. I decided to stay in Dublin rather than going to London to be with him at the Conrad Hotel, because I'd been away a lot and wanted some time with the family. On top of that, Michael was in the best position to talk about it all, since he'd been to all the meetings with Frank and could tell it as it was.

It was big news. The story – that I had been 'sacked' – was carried on the front pages of the newspapers and on all the main news bulletins. To me, 'sacked' means you've been dismissed there and then. To say that I was sacked was, I thought, just typical Fleet Street top-spin. The fact,

> **I wanted to go to Monza and reverse what had happened at Spa, where Jacques had taken four points away from me.**

the only fact, was that I would not be driving for Williams in 1997. But it was viewed as a hell of a slap in the face, and that indeed was how I took it – before I managed to push it out of my mind and settle down to the main job of winning the Italian Grand Prix and with it, I hoped, the championship. I wanted to go to Monza and reverse what had happened at Spa, where Jacques had taken four points away from me.

At Monza, of course, I had to face the press for the first time since the announcement the previous weekend. We organised a news conference which took place in Williams' part of the paddock club, instead of our usual smaller gathering on a Thursday afternoon at the motor-home. It was pretty gruelling. There were a lot of questions and a lot of things to say, but I did my best to get through it without being negative or unreasonable, simply because I really wanted to get it over with and get on with the racing. I explained how I felt, talked about the decision and my future, but there was not a lot I could say at that stage. I just wanted to have a bit of time to deal with the whole thing myself and, of course, I also wanted to get on with the weekend's work.

I'd had a lot of telephone calls from friends, people offering me advice, and some with very interesting propositions and offers. There were a few things that came along which I hadn't considered before, and which might have been quite good to have tried out! A lot of people were also very kind, and I was grateful to them all for their support and really wanted to perform to my absolute best once I got back to my car.

Monza is a wonderful place to go racing. The Italians are always so enthusiastic and this year there was another huge crowd and a typically passionate atmosphere. It is a circuit where, because of the long straights, we reduce the downforce as much as we can to get a maximum top speed of 220mph. But the key to a quick lap time at Monza is to jump over the chicanes. The problem this year, however, was that they'd been modified incorrectly to satisfy the motorcyclists who'd recently raced there. The net result was that the cars could use too much of the

> **I felt very composed and determined throughout practice and qualifying. I drove as well as I'd ever done, claiming pole position for the nineteenth time in my career.**

area behind the kerb itself and were deliberately cutting out whole sections of the track. In addition to that, the ground was being ripped up, exposing loose and thick layers of concrete which could then dislodge themselves and damage the cars.

This happened to Jacques on Friday, and resulted in him breaking the front wing of his car, something which is extremely dangerous on such a high-speed track as Monza. A television camera had worked loose off Jean Alesi's car last year and struck Gerhard Berger's with pretty serious consequences, and we were all aware of how perilous it would be to continue with the risk of these loose concrete kerbs at the chicanes breaking up when struck by the cars and then bouncing around the circuit. If one was to fly up and strike a car or driver, the potential outcome just didn't bear thinking about. So, at the end of the Friday morning session, Jacques, Gerhard and I went to see Roger Lane-Knott, and we agreed that temporary tyre barriers were the only sensible way to stop the cars from going over too much kerb at the chicanes. Something had to be done and we had to keep the cars off the kerbs. It wasn't a perfect solution, but we all agreed it was the best one in the circumstances.

I felt very composed and determined throughout

practice and qualifying. I drove as well as I'd ever done, claiming pole position for the nineteenth time in my career. Jacques was second fastest and took his position alongside me on the front row of the grid. It seemed the tyre barriers were doing their job, but I wasn't too happy with the fact that they were bolted to the ground, standing up like a solid lump of rubber, but on the other hand I knew it would have been just as dangerous to have loose tyres rolling around the track. We all agreed it was the right thing to do, they were bolted down and everyone tried to keep away from them. And they did – during qualifying and the warm-up. Unfortunately, the race was a completely different matter.

I knew that if I finished ahead of Jacques it would be very difficult for him to win the championship in the remaining two races. This thought was uppermost in my mind. I would have loved to have bagged the thing there and then; with regard to all that had happened over the previous week, the timing would have been perfect.

I made a very good start, and was being pretty aggressive to keep Jacques behind me as we went down to the first chicane. I blocked him, so he'd have to go the long way round, but I also had to deal with another threat. Jean Alesi had made a rocket-launcher of a start in his Benetton, and jumped from sixth place on the grid into the lead at the first corner. He was on my left, and when I looked in my mirror I could see that Jacques was on my right. I knew I couldn't defend against Alesi because he already had too much momentum, but I had to prevent other cars going down the inside, behind him, and at the same time not leave Jacques any room.

At the first chicane, with the tyres in place, there was simply no way anyone could cut across the kerbs. I knew that Jacques wouldn't make it through the corner unless he backed off, but I sensed that he wasn't going to budge. He was adamantly holding on to his line as I slipped through the chicane in second place behind Alesi. At the time I didn't see, or know, what had happened to Jacques, but later I discovered he went straight off and across the chicane. Alesi came out in front, I was second and Jacques was somewhere further back. That was good news as far as I was concerned – I was in a good position, and if Alesi

> **I could hardly believe it and I was thinking, 'Jesus, Jean! Please – just this once – back off!'**

went on to win the race, that was fine by me so long as I was in front of Jacques.

But that thought didn't last long. A little further round this hard-fought first lap, coming out of the second Lesmo corner, Alesi made a mistake and his car spun almost sideways as he struggled to regain control. I'd managed to get alongside him between the two Lesmos and outbraked him into the second. It was a ferocious duel. I knew Jacques would have a hard time getting past Alesi, so if I could put him between the two of us at that stage, I knew it would be a big help. But as we went into the Ascari chicane, I realised that Alesi had towed me all the way down the straight and, as I turned in, I could just see his front wheel coming along the inside of me. I could hardly believe it and I was thinking, 'Jesus, Jean! Please – just this once – back off!'

I was on the point of moving out of the way when I changed my mind and, instead, just leaned on him ever so gently. He reacted immediately, moving across to the left, and I knew that I had him – but it was a pretty dramatic moment. Then I began to pull away and settle into a rhythm, enjoying driving the car and leading the field. On about the fourth lap I got a pit signal telling me Jacques was fourth. At the time I thought it must have been a simple case of him having been passed – but whatever it was, it was encouraging news. I may have relaxed fractionally because I thought that all I needed to do now was to drive sensibly. But, on the next lap, I hit the tyres.

What I didn't know before this was that Jacques had hit the tyres already and was in dire straits, which was why he was fourth. His car had misaligned wheels. The tyres were starting to blister and it was very difficult for him to drive. This was to have serious repercussions for his hopes of scoring points, but equally, it was about to save my bacon!

I had no one but myself to blame for what happened. Sometimes, with Formula One cars, if you don't drive them hard, they can catch you out just as much as when they are on the limit. Whatever, I drifted too wide and hit the tyres. I didn't hit them hard, I just brushed them, but because they were bolted to the ground they did a lot of damage. The steering column was bent and the impact spun me round in the middle of the track. The engine stalled and I was left with nowhere to go. I got out of the car and just wanted to die.

I couldn't believe I'd made such a stupid mistake. I'd never done anything like that before. But it was my mistake – absolutely my mistake. I'd thrown it away, pure and simple. I set off to go back to the pits. It seemed a short distance when I was in the car driving at 200mph, but when I was walking back after doing something like that it seemed to take for ever. All the way, there were people clapping and cheering – as I said, the Italians are enthusiastic and knowledgeable – and I knew that they were happy because it meant Michael Schumacher was up to second place in his Ferrari. But, also, I think there was a lot of genuine appreciation being shown for my efforts. Inside, I was feeling absolutely sick with myself. But I knew that I had to bear up: it was my own fault. I just had to get back to the garage, pack up and get out of there.

It took me ten laps to get back to the garage, and the race was on lap fourteen by the time I got there. Jacques was coming out of the pits, which I thought was a bit odd. After my accident, I was convinced he was going to win the race, that he would beat the Ferraris and Alesi and, in my head, I was churning over the consequences. I was imagining there'd be only three points between us when we went to Estoril. I got back to the motor-home. All the press were there, naturally, and I just had to put on a brave face and own up – while all the time thinking, 'What's happening to Jacques?' I went into the motor-home to watch the race on television and was amazed, and relieved, to see that Jacques was in a worse state than I had been.

I still felt terrible. Georgie was there with me, and she'd so much wanted it all to be over. The whole championship had been just as stressful for her as it had for me, and there was nothing I could say except that it was my fault and that it was not to be, at least not on this weekend. As we sat there, we could see that Jacques was dropping down the field, out of the top six and making more pit-stops. His damaged car was rooting his tyres, and he needed new tyres all the time. He wasn't able to get back into the top six. Pedro Diniz, who'd been chastised severely by Jacques for nearly causing a big accident on Saturday, ended up driving his best race to finish sixth, keeping Jacques out of the points.

During the race, there were several heart-stopping moments. One came when Eddie Irvine dropped out in his Ferrari. I thought, 'Please, Eddie, don't do that,' because I believed that every time someone dropped out my championship lead would be cut by Jacques moving up a place. Apart from Jacques and me hitting the tyres there were several others, including Frentzen and, most famously, Michael Schumacher, who really clobbered them when he was leading the race. He got away with it, even though his hands came away from the steering wheel and he had to fight like mad to regain control of his car.

I was almost as relieved as he was that he did get away with it, because he went on to win the race. I'd never been so pleased to see Michael Schumacher win a race, apart from the previous one at Spa! I could hardly believe my luck. The outcome was that Jacques didn't score, and I still had my thirteen-point lead. To have come away from that accident, thinking I'd blown it in the biggest possible way, to finishing the afternoon closer to the championship, with one race fewer to the end of the season, was a strange sensation. But I was far from happy with myself, as I knew I'd messed up the race – and there was no getting away from the fact that I'd let a rare opportunity slip through my fingers.

At Monza, in 1992, Nigel Mansell had announced to the world that he was leaving Formula One to race in

> **But I was far from happy with myself, as I knew I'd messed up the race – and there was no getting away from the fact that I'd let a rare opportunity slip through my fingers.**

America, a decision that changed my life as much as his as it led directly to me being signed to race for Williams. This time around it was no different – only it was me who was moving on. Suffice it to say that, one way or another, I could always count on something big happening to me at Monza …

13 🏁 PORTUGAL

I left Monza on Sunday night, soon after the race was over, and flew to Austria while Georgie went home to Ireland. I'd been invited by Erwin Göllner several times to go mountain-climbing, but hadn't even been able to get to Austria since our first session back in January. With a test organised to take place at the new Österreichring (re-named the A1!) two days later, it seemed the perfect opportunity to accept. I spent Monday climbing and it was well worth the effort, a perfect way of winding down and helping to forget the Italian Grand Prix.

We got up quite early, left the hotel at about eight o'clock and, as part of my preparations for the next race at Estoril, went off to ascend this mountain I'd been told about. It was certainly more interesting than pedalling and rowing in a gym and made a welcome change, even if the word 'climbing' is perhaps a bit of an exaggeration.

The mountain reached an altitude of 1,800 metres and had snow on top, which contrasted somewhat with the weather at Monza the previous day. It took about one and a half hours to climb, which apparently was quite quick. It was more like hiking than true mountaineering, with picks and ropes and so on, but it was still demanding exercise and very rewarding, particularly when we reached the top. There, we met Jon Nicholson, who'd come up an easier way with his cameras. It was certainly memorable – and not only for the wonderful air, the views over Salzburg and the sense of exhilaration. As soon as we'd reached the top my mobile phone rang – it was Barry Sheene, calling from Australia to say hello and find out what was going on. I told him I was on top of a mountain in Austria – I'm not sure he believed me, but you could hardly blame him.

The following day I spent five hours mountain-biking around Salzburg and up more mountains, and then on Wednesday I went to Zeltweg, somewhat saddle-sore. There were about 5,000 people there for the test session, because it was the first time they'd seen Formula One cars there for quite a while. In fact, there were only three cars and drivers there in all – myself and the two McLarens, driven by David Coulthard and Mika Hakkinen – but the spectators didn't seem to mind at all, and they had an enjoyable day while I managed to get in some useful testing before flying home to Ireland.

Erwin came back to Dublin with me and we did four days' intensive training to make sure I was properly prepared for Estoril. We were in the gym for at least four hours each day and, after that, I felt confident I was as well prepared as I could possibly be for what I knew would be a very tough physical challenge in the Portuguese Grand Prix. I'd done enough laps there in the past to know it was hard on the neck and arms and that it was very important to be in top form, physically, as well as mentally.

The situation with regard to the championship was simple enough: if I finished in front of Jacques, I would win it. But I knew it wasn't actually that simple on the track. For a start, we were so competitive at Estoril that we were further ahead of our rivals than anywhere else we'd raced. I knew it was likely to be between the two of us right from the start. This was illustrated by qualifying, as I claimed pole by nine-thousandths of a second, no more than the equivalent of seventy-five centimetres on the track, before the rain came down and I could delight in having got my own back on him for what had happened at Spa. This time, it was Jacques who was unable to respond.

It may have been close, but it was immensely satisfying all the same. I was encouraged too by the big turnout of British fans, in the grandstand opposite the pits, who erupted with flags, hooters and plenty of shouting and noise in general every time I showed my face in the garage. It was obvious there were a lot of people in Estoril who had come from England, hoping and expecting me to sew up the title.

That was certainly my intention, but the problem for me was that the next guy behind me and Jacques on the grid was seven-tenths away; in other words, a lot slower. That was Jean Alesi, and he was ahead of Michael Schumacher, so it seemed to me that there wasn't going to be any way for me to finish ahead of Jacques other than by winning the race. It looked, on the performances in practice and qualifying, as if it was going to be down to the two of us.

I knew the kind of things that were going through people's minds, because I was thinking them too. I'd brought Georgie down to Portugal with me and, although it was never said, it was clearly felt that this could be it. This could be the one, the place where we could finish it all off. I kept trying to pull myself back to the realisation that I didn't actually have to win the race to become champion and that I'd still be in an exceptionally strong position if I finished second. I knew that would mean Jacques would have to win the next race, the last one in Japan, with me not scoring at all if he was to take the title. I didn't want it to go to the next race, though – I wanted to finish it off in Portugal.

I'd wanted it to be over at Monza, too, but had fouled it up and crashed and was carrying that thought in my mind as well. I knew that qualifying was vital because, psychologically, pole position gives you an edge as well as a better place to start from, on the cleaner side of the track. Assuming I made a good start and led Jacques on lap one, I should have been able to control the race. Pole gave me a lot of reasons to be optimistic.

There was a very strong feeling that we were about to see the championship decided, and I badly wanted to win the race, but I wasn't prepared to take any risks. Not after

> **I'd brought Georgie down to Portugal with me and, although it was never said, it was clearly felt that this could be it. This could be the one, the place where we could finish it all off.**

what had happened at Monza. But for Jacques, on the other hand, it was win or bust. He had to win and he had nothing to lose. I've been in his position in the past, and I knew that he had to commit everything. He had no choice.

I managed to stay focused through the weekend. I kept myself relaxed. I stayed on top of the job and remained as calm as I possibly could in order to be in the right frame of mind for the race. I kept my adrenaline in check to prevent being too pumped-up. You see it in all kinds of sports – it is so easy to do and an easy trap to fall into. You see golfers hit shots that go twenty yards further than they used to because they've got all this adrenaline running through them. I was acutely conscious of this, and I worked at containing myself at what I thought was just the right level of readiness for the race.

As I got into the car, before the race, the thought flashed though my head that in an hour and forty-five minutes I could be the world champion. I actually said to myself, 'The next time I climb out of this car, I want to be world champion!' It was my positive thought for the day! I felt I was perfectly prepared, calm, ready. I was on pole, so I'd been able to choose the pit-stops first, and I knew the right way to go was for a three-stop race. I also knew exactly what Jacques was doing. I'd chosen to try and stop before Jacques, to take advantage of everything I could.

The start was everything I could have hoped for. I got into the lead straight away, resisted a challenge from Jean Alesi (again!) and went for it. Jacques was down in fourth place and, I have to say, at that point I thought, 'This is it.'

I just wanted to stay in front, and I really did make a flying start. If anyone thought I was hard on Alesi, then all I can say is that I was utterly determined to take the road and get out into the clean air. I knew Jean was a threat. He'd made so many blinding starts during the season that I'd considered the possibility of him taking the lead at the start. But I felt that if he did that, it would have made it even more difficult for Jacques. I knew that it was important for me to stay ahead of Alesi, if I could, to put him between us, as at Monza. But Jacques was back behind Michael, also as at Monza – only this time his car was in perfect racing order.

> **As I got into the car, before the race, the thought flashed through my head that in an hour and forty-five minutes I could be the world champion.**

I fought very hard to keep the lead. After the first lap I drove at a pace which I thought was comfortable, but then I told myself that I needed to get moving. It was obvious that Jacques was going to come through, either at the pit-stops or at some other time, and I needed to open up a gap ahead of Alesi. The pit-wall was giving me signals of the times, and they told me the gap to Alesi was eleven seconds and the gap to Jacques was twelve. This indicated to me, though I did not know how he'd done it, that Jacques was now in front of Michael.

I knew the early part of the race would be relatively easy as long as Jacques was stuck in traffic, but that it would be much more difficult once Jacques got on to some clear road. That's why it was so important for me to press on and build up an advantage. The first pit-stop went well, but I knew Jacques would be running second as soon as Alesi made his scheduled stop, and that he'd be trying to close on me. This happened exactly as I'd expected, but what I'd not anticipated – or wanted – was to lose five seconds of my hard-won twelve-second lead through trouble with back-markers.

I was coming down to the first corner where there were two cars deeply involved in their own fight, trying to overtake one another. I didn't know who they were at the time, except that one was an Arrows and the other was a Tyrrell. They were weaving all over the place. One had just come out of the pits and the other was holding him up by weaving, changing his line, and they were chopping back and forth like they were on a slalom course. It was wacky races, and I just knew that if I tried to pass I'd run the risk of them driving into me. They had no idea that the leader was right behind them. In one lap, my lead was cut back to only seven seconds.

By the time we made our second pit-stops, my lead was down to three seconds and Jacques was coming at me like a train. I decided that the best thing for me to do was to defend rather than try to up my pace, as it was clear he was charging hard and throwing caution to the wind. I was not going to be forced into making a mistake, so I elected to sit there, in the lead, driving at the pace I wanted – and no faster.

> **It was wacky races, and I just knew that if I tried to pass I'd run the risk of them driving into me. They had no idea that the leader was right behind them.**

He was on my tail for a couple of laps, but I was able to improve my advantage a little, to open up a gap of about two seconds, knowing that the third pit-stops were coming up and I'd need every inch of my lead. I knew also that I needed a quick in-lap and a quick out-lap, and I was hoping it would all go well when, on my in-lap, I came upon David Coulthard, who had a puncture, and was limping back to the pits with his car on three wheels. At first I thought his car was damaged – it had the look of a car about to do something erratic – so I gave him a very wide berth. As I went round the last corner, I was concerned that something might fall off his car or that he might spin right in front of me. My caution again cost me time I could ill-afford to lose.

The stop itself went absolutely perfectly until I was ready to go out again, and David came trundling down the pit-lane with his puncture. Carl Gaden, our chief mechanic and the man with the lollipop, had the job of checking the lane to make sure it was clear before he could release me and, of course, he had no choice but to hold me there until the path was clear. That cost me another second to Jacques, but I didn't realise it would be so damaging at the time. My out-lap felt like a good one, and the car felt so good that as I came down the straight again at the end of the next lap, I simply couldn't believe it when I saw Jacques popping out of the pit-lane in front of me. It was incredible. I had to do a double take. He was barely a quarter of a second ahead of me, but he was in front and that was all he needed. He might just as well have been a lap ahead. I didn't want to believe it was him and, at first, I thought it was a Tyrrell, but the Rothmans decal on the rear wing confirmed my worst fears.

I suppose I knew in that second that it was going to be almost impossible for me to win the race now that he was in front. To be half a second or so ahead of someone on that circuit is a very different thing from being half a second behind. You just can't pass anyone, particularly if the two cars are of similar performance ability, without taking a massive risk. But I just had to try and stick on his tail in the hope that there might be an opportunity. So I pushed, but he'd obviously been extra motivated from moving ahead of me. I pushed for about three or four laps, but I wasn't fast enough to make any impression, or enough of an impression, and I resigned myself to the reality that I'd simply have to bring the car home without mishap – and wait until Suzuka to try and settle the championship.

But the drama, or at least my contribution to it, was not over yet. With about fourteen or fifteen laps to go, the pits came on the radio to me and told me they'd detected that the temperature was rising in the clutch. I knew this usually meant a problem with the clutch release bearing, as we'd had some trouble with this in previous races and in testing. I knew too that if it isn't identified and rectified quickly, the clutch can heat up so much that the fly-wheel expands, hits the crank-shaft sensor which, in turn, cuts out the electrics on the car. In other words, it could cause me to stop and retire from the race.

This time I was lucky. The boys in the pits had spotted the trouble on the car's garage telemetry early enough to warn me about it, and they advised me to go to another setting on the clutch, which meant de-activating the clutch release bearing and therefore stopping it from getting any hotter. This may have saved my race, but it left me with another unknown added to the overall equation, as I was left running without a clutch at all, which can cause problems for the gearbox.

Fortunately we'd done some testing for just such an eventuality, and so I was able to make it to the finish, score the six points I needed for second place and breathe a sigh of relief. Of course, I was disappointed not to have won, but I was also lucky to have got to the end of the race at all. When my car was examined, it was found that the clutch was right on the edge of collapse, and I was very lucky to have finished.

It was a very strange feeling to stand on that podium. I couldn't help feeling that I'd let another good opportunity to win the race and the championship pass me by. But on the other hand, I knew also that I'd done the right thing and guaranteed myself the best chance of reaching my ultimate goal. I knew I was no longer fighting to win races. I was driving to win the championship, and that was a wholly different matter.

It may have been disappointing, particularly for the many British supporters who had travelled to Estoril, but at least I knew exactly what lay ahead for me. The championship had gone all the way to the last race, at Suzuka, and I knew that I would need only one point, while Jacques had to win and then hope for some help from me. His job was going to be ten times more difficult than mine, but with one more race to go, there was still a

> **I knew I was no longer fighting to win races. I was driving to win the championship, and that was a wholly different matter.**

chance that just about anything could happen. A tense interlude could be an appropriate description of the gap between races, but having waited my whole life to win the championship, I felt certain I could bear the three weeks that lay ahead before the final race in Japan.

14 🏁 JAPAN

In the event I needn't have worried about how I was going to fill the time between races. On Sunday night, rather than stay for the traditional end–of–European–season celebrations, combined with Williams' constructors' championship party in the seaside town of Cascais, I opted to dash home to see my children for thirty-six hours, as I knew I was heading for a busy week.

On Wednesday I was back testing at Estoril. On Thursday I flew to England to do my deal with TWR Arrows. Friday I was announcing my new contract to the stunned ranks of the media in London, and then I had time to spend the weekend with my family and friends in Kent. On Monday I flew to the Paris Motor Show, ful-filling one of my obligations to Renault, then I went back to Tom Walkinshaw's impressive new factory at the

TWR Arrows headquarters in Leafield to meet more journalists before flying home on Tuesday. That gave me all of Wednesday in my own home with my family, before leaving for Hong Kong on Thursday evening in order to be properly adjusted to the time difference for Suzuka the following week. Believe me, there was absolutely no time to bite my nails.

It was the strangest feeling leaving home on Thursday. When I returned I would either be world champion or the 'other thing', the unthinkable alternative. One thing was sure, though, my children probably wouldn't give a hoot either way. I saw them off to school and left for my appointment with destiny.

On my first night in Hong Kong I slept for fourteen hours. I obviously needed it. Georgie joined me on the Sunday, and we had a few days together doing all the usual tourist things, but also visiting her old home in the New Territories, where she had spent her early teen years. We avoided discussing Formula One quite easily, and had a great time relaxing. But Wednesday was D-Day: time to ship out to Japan and start the final countdown to the last and decisive Grand Prix of this long and incident-filled season. The last Grand Prix in a Williams car for me, too – although that hardly entered into my head at that particular time.

When I arrived at the circuit, it was clear to me that I was now part of an inexorable chain of events. I had a strong feeling of being sucked along towards the start of the race and the outcome I'd been waiting for. I put myself on autopilot and just followed the routine of the other fifteen races of the season, knowing I had a job to do.

I didn't want to be burdened by the magnitude of the significance of the race. I knew there were only two ways it could go … and, in some ways, I viewed it as a relief. At last, whatever was going to happen was now going to happen. But, from the moment I arrived at the track, I could see that this race would be different. I could see it in the looks on the faces of so many other people, their faces betraying their emotions.

The last race of the season usually has an 'end-of-term' feel to it, and, for that reason, everyone sports a big smile because they know there's just one more to go. But this time the smiles were few and far between. I could see another look on their faces. They were thinking, 'How does he look? How's he coping?' But I always knew it would be like that. It was my job to avoid being upset, which could so easily have happened if I'd taken any notice of the comments people made. Some said things like, 'Go for it, Damon!', while others just issued a half-baked 'Oh my God, I hope he's not going to blow it' type of attitude.

The atmosphere was pregnant with anticipation. This, we all knew, was the race where the championship would be decided.

I didn't think Jacques would have any problems with the circuit; as Mika Hakkinen said, after the race, it is, along with Spa, the best race track in the world. It's longer than most and has a lot of long, fast and dangerous corners. Although I agree it is a great track to drive on, I have to say also that I certainly don't feel comfortable with Suzuka's level of safety.

Jacques, of course, had only one course of action open to him, which was to take all the risks and not hold back in any way. He couldn't afford to be conservative, as I could, but my situation also gave me too many options. I could have done almost anything, including starting, as someone suggested, from the back row of the grid to avoid the first corner problems. All I needed was to finish sixth and, of course, it was possible to start last and go through and finish in the points. But it didn't take long to discount that particular idea. It would have been quite a public relations challenge to explain to the British public why I'd qualified on the back row! And, if it had gone badly wrong, I think I'd have felt very stupid indeed. Another option was to throw caution to the wind, go all out for pole and then try and dominate the race. Or I could have gone for something in between. Sometimes, there are just too many options to choose from!

When I arrived at the track I said to the press that I hadn't decided on my tactics yet, but one thing I was certain about – I wanted to be on the front row of the grid. I knew that if I started on the second row with the likes of Michael, Jean or Gerhard in front, I'd be in danger because they had nothing to lose. They'd all want to go all-out for a win in the final race of the year.

Early on Friday morning I had a dream, in which I had won the championship and Jacques had won the race. Everyone was happy and celebrating. Then I woke up – and it wasn't Sunday but only Friday, and I realised how much work still had to be done. I thought that was a particularly cruel trick for my mind to play on me. Still, I now knew what I had to do to feel that good again, and I headed off to the circuit with extra motivation.

Jacques took care of his side of things by being quick all the time on Friday and Saturday. I took a little more care than usual on those two days up to the final run in qualifying, when I pushed myself to get on the front row. It would have been very satisfying to have taken pole, but

I wasn't prepared to risk everything for it. I remembered what had happened to Nigel Mansell at Suzuka in 1987, when he turned up with a chance of winning the championship, but put himself out of the last two races by having an accident. Suzuka is the kind of place where, if you do have an accident, it's almost certain to be a big one.

It was raining a lot of the time too, but during the wet weather on Saturday morning I was two seconds clear of everyone else. At least I knew I had a good wet set-up. I wasn't worried about driving in the wet at Suzuka either, having won there in 1994, but I still didn't relish the idea. I knew I'd have a big advantage if it was wet, but so many other factors made it much more risky.

My plan for qualifying was to do two timed laps on each run. Jacques had put the hammer down and pushed the limits all the time. Before my last run, he was 1.5 seconds quicker than me, but I knew I hadn't really pushed myself hard. However, I was fourth on the grid, which was where I didn't want to be, so I decided my last run had to be a bit more do-or-die and I left it until two and a half minutes to go before leaving the garage. As I went out Adrian Newey came on the radio and said, 'Don't stall it,' which was just the sort of thing you don't say at that particular moment. I didn't stall it at all and, in reply, all I offered was a dry 'Thank you, Adrian.' As if I needed any more pressure!

So off I went to try and improve my position, a task that is much easier when there's nothing pressing on your mind. The times when I've driven my best have always been when I've been totally free and have loosened up and just enjoyed it. I told myself it was time to switch into that mode, but I still couldn't let go completely – I had to make sure I didn't end up watching the race on television from a hospital bed. It was with those thoughts, and in that state of mind, that I went out and found the extra second and a bit I needed to put the car on the front row of the grid. And, in now-traditional Hill style, I left it to the very last second.

When I climbed out of my car I went to see Jacques. He seemed a little unhappy. I expected him to be jumping up and down because he'd got pole position, but he appeared to be burdened by the fact that I'd popped up on the front row right at the last second. He wasn't going to shake me off easily now – I said as much in the media conference afterwards. I didn't mind being out-qualified by Jacques, because I was only concerned about being at the front, to see where he was and have an opportunity to get into the first corner ahead of him. He knew that, and he was needled. There was no question about it.

He'd tried his best. He'd pushed out the boat and I was still with him – and that was all I needed to do. Not only that, but we both knew that the front row of the grid at Suzuka is slightly strange because pole position, on the right, is only a little cleaner than second position on the left. The first corner is a very fast right-hander where you don't have to get completely in front of the car to your left. You just have to be alongside, and there's no way the driver on the left can do anything about it. You can use all the road you like on the exit – the other driver just has to back off.

I was in the right place; there was no doubt about it. I'd kept the pressure on Jacques, and while he kept on saying to the press that I was the one under pressure, I knew that because he kept throwing that one into my court it indicated that he was feeling the pressure just as

> **Qualifying lifted me a lot, and in that moment when I secured my place on the front row, I felt I dealt with the whole burden of what I was about to do. I felt sure now that I would be champion on Sunday.**

much as me. Although he didn't appear to be too concerned about the championship, I knew he was. I knew he was just like the rest of us, and would be clinging on to the hope that it might still happen. I could see from his attitude after qualifying that he was affected by the possibility of not winning the championship or the race. His body language suggested that he was deflated, and I guessed that it was down to one or both of these reasons.

Qualifying lifted me a lot, and in that moment when I secured my place on the front row, I felt I dealt with the whole burden of what I was about to do. I felt sure now that I would be champion on Sunday.

My good work in qualifying made Saturday evening much easier for me. I'd flown out a few of my closest friends and supporters to help take my mind off the job. I tried the best I could to wind down in the evenings, and I must say everyone did a great job of smiling every time they saw me – a factor which did not go unnoticed. It was great for my morale and much appreciated; the last thing I wanted was a lot of nervous people around me just then.

But when I went to bed on Saturday night I couldn't sleep at all. It had nothing to do with jet-lag: I just lay in bed until at least midnight, which under normal circumstances would have been okay, but we had to get up at

6.30 in the morning, which meant it felt like a very short night. I don't normally need a lot of sleep at race meetings, but my body was crying out for it, pleading for a release from the tension.

I was able to remind myself that it was my last night with all this championship thing going through my head, and I knew that when I woke up on Sunday morning it was going to be the conclusive day of the year. After all those nights of not being able to relax properly, it was great to know, when it came, that this was it – the final day. Not possibly; not probably; but absolutely and definitely the last day. And that put a real spring into my step on Sunday morning – even though it was chucking it down with rain outside.

The warm-up was done in the wet, but eventually the sun came out and it was beautiful – the first time I can remember the weather being so warm and perfect at Suzuka. Although my grid position was the last thing to dry up, much to my increasing anxiety, finally the sun dried out everything. My state of mind was perfect too. I'd never felt so balanced before a race. I wasn't too relaxed, but not too tense, either. I was fully charged. I'd hit it perfectly in terms of readiness for the start and I was able to try and impart some calm to my engineers and mechanics, to help them to stay cool.

I said 'See you later' to Georgie as always, gave her a kiss and headed into the garage. A few minutes before we left to go on to the grid, about half an hour before the race, I went over to Jacques' mechanics and wished them luck for the race. I don't know what happened, but I started to get emotional. I suddenly realised it was my last race for Williams and something just seemed to happen. I said goodbye to them and had to pull myself together a bit and get back into the car, get myself back in the right frame of mind and, by the time I had crossed the garage, I was okay again.

All of my mechanics were decked out in London Rowing Club caps, blue with white stripes, and that helped to keep me light-hearted as we went to the grid. I didn't see much of Patrick Head, but he came to me on the grid when I was in the car. It's almost been a tradition for Patrick to come and see me before a race and give me some pearl of wisdom. Usually he'd come up and say something very obvious, like 'try and drive on the track' or 'don't forget to make a good start'. I might as well have told him: 'Don't forget to put all the fuel in'! It was just his way of covering all the possibilities. But this time, after years of giving me all sorts of advice, he came up and said, 'I don't think I need to give you any advice for this one, Damon. Good luck – and see you later.'

Tony Jardine, the BBC's pit-lane reporter, also spoke to me while I was on the grid, and I was very conscious of the feeling that I was standing in Suzuka, on the other side of the world, in broad daylight and in warm sunshine while everyone at home was just getting out of bed in the middle of the night to watch the race. I was aware then of all the people back at home sitting on the edge of their seats, palms sweating, biting their nails – but I knew it was going to be worth it. I felt confident.

The tension built up as usual, but we proceeded as normal and completed the final warm-up lap. Then, lo and behold, there was a delayed start. It turned out to be David Coulthard, which I didn't realise at the time, but they got on with the re-start pretty quickly. It was one of those things I could have done without, but the delay didn't last long and we were soon back into the routine again. Finally the re-start came. I watched the lights carefully, and when they went out, I went – and Jacques didn't!

> **Finally the re-start came. I watched the lights carefully, and when they went out, I went – and Jacques didn't!**

At first I thought my car was going to bog down on me, but I actually made one of the best starts of my life. It was so good that, after the race, Denis Chevrier, the Renault engineer in charge of my car, gave me a telemetry print-out of it and wrote on the back: 'If you repeat a start like that one often, we will have to battle together next season. All the best, Denis.'

I was ahead of Jacques, out in front, and I knew what that meant. I thought back to Monza and Estoril, with him down in fourth, and told myself, 'This time I'm staying here.' I tried to drive with as much exuberance as I could, but I could not rely on my instincts and detach myself from what was going on. I drove the first few laps mechanically, not naturally, and Gerhard Berger closed up on me. I had set myself the objective of sliding into the rhythm of the race, rather than doing what I did at Monza and relaxing too much. This allowed Gerhard to get close and, actually, he nearly took me off.

I saw him coming from 130-R, the fast left-hander before the chicane. He went for it and I could hear his engine noise so close it reminded me of my days in bike racing. I shut the door on him and the next time I looked he was a long way back. He took avoiding action, hit the kerb – not me – and that was it. It was only when I saw it on television afterwards that I realised how near he'd been to taking me. After that I controlled things without any problems. I kept Mika Hakkinen at a safe distance and, in the knowledge that Jacques seemed to be stuck down in fourth place, worked at staving off all those premature thoughts of victory which kept trying desperately to come into my head and distract me. Luckily, there's nothing like Suzuka, as a race circuit, to keep your mind on the job.

My pit-stops went well, although the first one was extended by a delay and my lead was cut. The last two stints were only seventeen laps each, and I pushed hard on the middle stint to retain and extend my advantage. However, this was definitely a race to be won at the slowest possible speed – à la Fangio – as long as Jacques was in the race, but with fourteen laps to go Tim Preston gave me the surprise news: 'Jacques is out, Damon! Jacques is out!'

That was it. Championship decided. I had done it! I was world champion! All I could think was that I must have had an angel looking over me that day. It all went my way: absolutely everything was too good to be true, and to cap it all I could clinch the race victory as well. For two laps I drove like a zombie, watching the road fly beneath me, unable to work out if it was real. I realised I could just stop the car if I wanted to, climb out and walk away, and the result would be the same. The car could break down, and it wouldn't matter one bit. At one point I thought I could crash, end up in hospital with a leg in plaster and still be the champion, which would have been somewhat unusual!

Then my mind switched to all my friends and supporters. What must they be doing now? I could picture Georgie surrounded by everyone back in the pits, celebrating already, with me still out there with fourteen laps to go. 'Wait for me!' I thought. I could imagine Murray Walker going into berserk overdrive as he relayed the news to Britain; I could almost hear him in the car!

Then I thought about Frank and Patrick, and Adrian and all the boys in the team, and my mind focused back on the race. We'd come to Suzuka to win, not to hand victory to whoever was second. There would be reason for us all to celebrate if I could finish off the job properly. Winning is even more satisfying if it is emphatic, and I was damned if I was going to let Michael Schumacher win, after all our battles. Besides, he was about to become the ex-world champion – he might as well come second in the race as well! There could be no other just outcome, so I put my foot down and pressed on to the finish.

Suddenly driving my car became a task so simple I was able to reel off the remaining laps and think about what I was going to say in the press conference directly after the race. It was as if the car was driving itself. On the penultimate lap I made a diving pass towards the pit-wall, just to give them all a fright – I was having fun at their expense, as I knew they'd be wondering what the hell I was playing at, but I was past caring at that point. Michael had backed off, knowing he'd be unable to catch me, so I had about six seconds in hand for the last lap.

As I came through the final corner I shouted to the team over the radio, 'This one's for everyone at Williams. This win's for you!' Then, as I rounded the corner, I could see the man with the chequered flag – and the whole pit-wall was like the Hanging Gardens of Babylon, with people, flags and a sign which read 'Damon Hill World Champion 1996' held out by the team. I slowed down and tried to pass right under the sign so I could see all the faces of the Williams crew; see them for the last time from the cockpit of one of their cars. In Adelaide in 1993, Joe Ramirez of McLaren had said to Ayrton Senna before the start of his last race for the team, 'If you win this one, Ayrton, I will love you for ever' – and Ayrton did win it. Now I was doing the same for my team.

In Formula One, where the talk is mostly of money, contractual obligations, strained relationships, Machiavellian antics and selfishness, it is hard to believe that more often than not we do have fun and enjoy doing well together as a team. In 1996 we'd worked better together than ever before, but of course I can only talk about my four seasons with them, in a team with a long history of success.

It was always going to be a temporary home for me, whereas for everyone from Frank and Patrick down, Williams Grand Prix Engineering offers something much longer-term, and in the context of the team's history and the contribution of those who have been with Williams far longer than me, it may sound presumptuous to be calling it 'my team'. But I have lived with Williams since 1991, when I became a test driver for them, and whenever I've been in the car I have always felt an obligation to give whatever I could, to repay the hours and hours of work and dedication with results. This was never more true than at Suzuka this year. I doubt whether I could ever have equalled the place in their hearts that Ayrton

> **As I came through the final corner I shouted to the team over the radio, 'This one's for everyone at Williams. This win's for you!'**

enjoyed at McLaren, but then Ayrton was in a different league altogether. All I will say is that I'll never forget my friends at Williams, and all the truly world-shattering events we have been through together.

I will remember those nights in the test-track office at Estoril in January, when after seven days of solid testing it seemed as though we were all going mad, and the slightest, stupidest thing would set us all off and double us up with laughter. I will remember sitting in an outdoor jacuzzi fully clothed at four in the morning with all my mechanics, drinking champagne after winning at Melbourne at the start of the season. I will remember sitting under the awning of the Williams motor-home in 1994 after winning the British Grand Prix, with Frank and Ginny Williams and my trophy, and all the fans, and the long summer evening drawing to a close as I signed, signed and signed my name over and over again with a huge grin on my face that wouldn't go away. I swear Frank was welling up too as Ginny put her arm around him.

I will remember the emotion in the team when I won in Spain in 1994, the first win after Ayrton's death. I will remember Frank's quiet words of support when no one was looking, and Patrick's outrageously obvious statements before I drive, such as 'There's rain coming from the sky' (Imola, 1995).

I will remember being a test driver, and getting support and advice from Nigel Mansell, whose career had inspired me ever since I'd been there to watch him win his first victory at Brands Hatch in 1985. I will remember being team-mates with Nigel, Alain and Ayrton, and being able to see their different approaches to the job.

I will remember working with Adrian Newey, who to the best of my knowledge has never raced himself, but who is able to understand what a driver needs from a car with uncanny precision, and who also possesses a talent for design and aerodynamics which in my opinion puts him into the Colin Chapman league, quite apart from being a faithful ally and friend, for which I thank him enormously.

I will remember working with Renault Sport, who have consistently provided the most reliable and

> **"I will remember being a test driver, and getting support and advice from Nigel Mansell, whose career had inspired me ever since I'd been there to watch him win his first victory at Brands Hatch in 1985."**

236

competitive F1 race engines for the last eight seasons and who have convinced me that it is possible for French and English people to work together – as long as they provide the best cuisine in the paddock. One of my best memories is of Christian Contzen, head of Renault Sport, and Bernard Dudot, the technical director, singing 'Michelle' with a karaoke machine at a pre-race dinner – traditionally held by Williams for all the Renault team – at Adelaide in 1993. They sang a duet in front of their amazed colleagues, who weren't at all used to seeing their bosses exposing themselves so readily to self-ridicule as we are in England. They naturally sang the French bit beautifully, but then had to face each other and take turns to sing, 'I love you, I love you, I *loooooove* you,' which was quite possibly the funniest thing I have ever seen in my life.

But it is the excellence of the Williams workforce which is the key to their success. The 220 people at Grove collectively produce the finest racing car in the world. In the whole of the season, Jacques and I only had one chassis design-related problem each which prevented us from finishing a race. These are all the reasons why I was eager to dedicate the race to the team.

But I had settled my debt to Williams. Now was the time to give myself a pat on the back. After passing the pits I knew I had only the slowing-down lap to be alone, to allow all the tension of the race, the weekend, the months – even the years – to escape. It is one of the unusual features of our sport that because our faces are hidden away in crash helmets and, by necessity, we have to complete a slowing-down lap, our most triumphant and ecstatic moments are almost totally private. But I don't mind sharing the experience in these pages, and admitting that I cried with joy and relief all the way back to the pit-lane.

When I reached the *parc fermé*, I sat in the car for a few extra seconds. I knew it was probably the last time I was going to be sitting in a Williams car in such circumstances. As I climbed out Michael and Mika shook my hand and congratulated me. Then I went to see Georgie by the railings, and I gave her a big sweaty hug before we went up to the podium.

It was so perfect to win the race and the championship on the same day that way. To be on top of the podium, for all the right reasons, and not have to be invited to join three other guys up there. I enjoyed the fact that it was Michael behind me at the finish, because racing against someone like him is a real challenge. But it was the right way to end, having won the race, standing on top of the podium as champion.

Quite often people have said I look too serious on the podium. Sometimes, in the past, I've looked like that because I've been trying to stop myself from crying. It is such an emotional moment up there, such a big release, and when you hear them playing the national anthem it inspires great pride. I feel proud and privileged to have had that moment. I looked down and I could see Georgie and all my friends, the team, everyone I knew from the F1 paddock – and they were all looking up with great big smiles on their faces.

I was thoroughly doused in champagne. So was Adrian Newey, who had come up to the podium. It was the start of the party and I felt intoxicated already just from the fumes of my champagne-soaked overalls and the joy of having won. It was an extraordinary feeling. I told the news conference that I felt as if I was on a rocket that was just about to take off, if it hadn't already done so. I had achieved the very highest goal I could as a racing driver. I was on top of the world.

The partying started almost immediately, and as the race finished at four in the afternoon, it was going to be a long party! I followed the traditional post-Suzuka fashion by singing the night away in a karaoke cabin, but I peaked too soon. I was in bed at one, but then woke up at four in the morning in a panic. I thought this was my

Groundhog Day dream, and that I was back to Friday morning again. I got up and went outside to see if it was all real. I wanted to check I really was there at Suzuka, that it really was Monday morning.

It was quiet, raining, and beautiful, as I started to soak up the realisation that I really was world champion. I felt, after such a long time in my cocoon of exclusively championship thoughts, that I had been released. I felt free. I felt alive. I felt fab.

> **I had achieved the very highest goal I could as a racing driver. I was on top of the world.**

Warner Books now offers an exciting range of quality titles by both established and new authors. All of the books in this series are available from:

    Little, Brown and Company (UK),
    P.O. Box 11,
    Falmouth,
    Cornwall TR10 9EN.

Fax No: 01326 317444.
Telephone No: 01326 372400
E-mail: books@barni.avel.co.uk

Payments can be made as follows: cheque, postal order (payable to Little, Brown and Company) or by credit cards, Visa/Access. Do not send cash or currency. UK customers and B.F.P.O. please allow £1.00 for postage and packing for the first book, plus 50p for the second book, plus 30p for each additional book up to a maximum charge of £3.00 (7 books plus).

Overseas customers including Ireland, please allow £2.00 for the first book plus £1.00 for the second book, plus 50p for each additional book.

NAME (Block Letters) ....

....

ADDRESS ....

....

....

☐ I enclose my remittance for ....

☐ I wish to pay by Access/Visa Card

Number ⬚⬚⬚⬚⬚⬚⬚⬚⬚⬚⬚⬚⬚⬚⬚⬚

Card Expiry Date ⬚⬚⬚⬚